ML

29 July 1999

RATIONAL CHOICE

Rational Choice

Michael Allingham
Magdalen College
Oxford

First published in Great Britain 1999 by
MACMILLAN PRESS LTD
Houndmills, Basingstoke, Hampshire RG21 6XS and London
Companies and representatives throughout the world

A catalogue record for this book is available from the British Library.

ISBN 0–333–74512–4

 First published in the United States of America 1999 by
ST. MARTIN'S PRESS, INC.,
Scholarly and Reference Division,
175 Fifth Avenue, New York, N.Y. 10010

ISBN 0–312–22446–X

Library of Congress Cataloging-in-Publication Data
Allingham, Michael.
Rational choice / Michael Allingham.
p.   cm.
Includes bibliographical references and index.
ISBN 0–312–22446–X (cloth)
1. Rational choice theory.   I. Title.
HM495.A45   1999
301'.01—dc21
99–21114
CIP

This book is printed on paper suitable for recycling and made from fully managed and
sustained forest sources.

10   9   8   7   6   5   4   3   2   1
08   07   06   05   04   03   02   01   00   99

Printed and bound in Great Britain by
Antony Rowe Ltd, Chippenham, Wiltshire

'Choice is deliberate desire.'

Aristotle

Contents

Preface   ix
Symbols   xi

Introduction   1

1 Choice   7

Choice Problems   7
Reasonable Choice   9
The Expansion and Contraction Axioms   12
Rational Choice   15
The Congruence Axiom   17
Preference Revelation   20
The Extension Axiom   22
Utility   26
An Overview   28

2 Uncertainty   31

Uncertainty Problems   31
Rationality and Expected Utility   33
The Substitution Axiom   37
The Continuity Axiom   40
The Expected Utility Property   44
Subjective Probability   46
State-Independent Utility   49

3 Risk   53

Number Lotteries   53
Risk Aversion   55
The Probability Risk Premium   58
The Outcome Risk Premium   61
Comparative Risk Aversion   64

4 Strategy **71**

Strategy Problems 71
Rationality and Rationalisable Acts 74
The Consistency Axiom 76
Dominance 79
Iteratively Undominated Acts 81
Equilibrium in Beliefs 83
Equilibrium in Acts 86

5 Knowledge **89**

Knowledge Functions 89
Self-Evident Sets 92
Knowledge Partitions 94
Mutual Knowledge 98
Common Knowledge 99
Common Knowledge and Self-Evident Sets 102
Knowledge and Choice Problems 105
Knowledge and Rationality 106

6 Society **111**

Social Choice Problems 111
Information Requirements 113
Responsiveness Requirements 116
Admissible and Acceptable Rules 119
Reasonable and Rational Rules 119
Acceptable Reasonable Rules 121
Admissible Rational Rules 125

Appendix: Sets and Numbers 129

References 137

Index 141

Preface

The primary purpose of this book is to develop the theory of rational choice in a simple framework in which the problems of pure choice, choice under uncertainty, strategic choice and social choice are unified. A secondary purpose is to comment on some aspects of attitudes to risk, as a digression on the second of these problems, and of the concept of knowledge, as a digression on the third. The book aims not to treat these problems exhaustively but rather to illuminate the common thread which runs through them. Although new results, or new demonstrations of existing results, are obtained such novelty is incidental: the central aim of the book is that of simplification and unification.

The approach is axiomatic: that is, abstract axioms which are intended to capture the essence of various aspects of rationality are formulated and their implications explored. Although the approach is abstract, technicalities are kept to a minimum. To this end the theory is developed in the simplest framework which provides interesting results: for example, all choice sets are taken to be finite or, at most, countable. The only mathematics which is used is that of simple operations on finite sets and on the rational numbers. No recourse is made to the real numbers or to mathematical analysis.

The core chapters on pure choice, choice under uncertainty and strategic choice are developed from three lectures delivered in the University of Oxford. The book was completed during a period of leave generously granted by the President and Fellows of Magdalen College.

MICHAEL ALLINGHAM

Symbols

{...}	Set
:	Such that
∈	Element
∉	Not element
⊂	Subset
∪	Union
∩	Intersection
\	Difference
×	Product
#	Cardinality
(...)	Array
≽	Relation (binary)
~	Symmetric component of ≽
≻	Asymmetric component of ≽
=	Equal
≠	Not equal
≥	At least as great
>	Greater
+	Addition
−	Subtraction
·	Multiplication
/	Division
$\sum[...]$	Summation (also $\sum$)
N	Natural numbers
Q̸	Rational numbers (nonnegative)
I̸	Unit interval (closed rational)
[...]	Degenerate probability
< ... >	Compound probability

xi

Introduction

Rational choice theory is a branch of logic: it provides criteria for assessing the consistency of choices and for deriving new choices from existing ones. It originates, as does logic itself, in the work of Aristotle.

For Aristotle, rational choice is central to the goal of life: eudaimonia, or living and faring well. However, it is instrumental in this: rationality is seen as an instrument for achieving ends which are not themselves determined by reason. Aristotle, in the *Nichomachean Ethics*, supports this position as follows. First, choice is a result of deliberation: 'the same thing is deliberated upon and is chosen'. Second, this deliberation concerns means rather than ends: 'we deliberate not about ends but about means'. And third, these ends are determined by wishes: 'wish relates rather to the end, choice to the means' (1980 translation, pp. 54–7). These three observations together imply that 'choice is deliberate desire' or, more fully, that 'choice is desire and reasoning with a view to an end' (p. 139).

This instrumental conception of choice is shared by modern philosophers. For example, Hume, in the *Treatise*, makes a clear separation between means and ends, or reason and passion, in his assertion that 'reason is, and ought only to be the slave of the passions'. Passions are neither reasonable nor unreasonable, reason entering the picture only when passions are translated by choice into action: 'a passion can never, in any sense, be call'd unreasonable' (1740, pp. 415–16). Mill, Bentham and other utilitarians, who see the fulfilment or otherwise of all passions as being reducible to the single dimension of utility, make the same separation. Choosing rationally becomes equivalent to maximising utility: that is, to seeking the greatest fulfilment of pre-existing passions.

There are three components of Aristotle's conception of choice as 'desire and reasoning with a view to an end': choice, being what we do; desire, being what we prefer; and

1

deliberation, or logic, which connects choice to desire. My choice is rational, or supported by reason, if it coheres with what I prefer.

A basic requirement for my choice to cohere with what I prefer is that there is some interpretation of the relation 'is at least as good as' according to which the outcome that I choose is at least as good as all others. If this is the case then we consider my choice to be reasonable. Reasonableness, however, does not ensure rationality: the relation 'at least as good as' may lack internal consistency. My choice is rational only if this relation is consistent. If this obtains we can assign numbers (which we may call utilities) to outcomes in such a way that the outcome which I choose is that with the highest utility. In Chapter 1 we characterise the choices which cohere with preferences in both the basic and the stronger senses: that is, we specify axioms which are necessary and sufficient for choice to be reasonable, and which are necessary and sufficient for choice to be rational and thus for us to be able to assign utilities.

Instead of specifying that choice is over outcomes we could equivalently specify that choice is over actions and that each action determines an outcome. We would then consider choice to be rational if the action which is chosen is that whose associated outcome has the highest utility. As an extension to this framework we now consider the case where there are a number of possible environments, or descriptions of the world, defined in such a way that precisely one will occur. In this framework an outcome is determined by the environment as well as by an action. We may consider the environment to be chosen randomly by 'Nature': I do not know what the environment will be but I do know the probability of each environment occurring. This means that I know the probability of each outcome given my action. As we can assign utilities to outcomes it follows that for any given action I can calculate, using the probabilities of the outcomes given that action, the mean of the utilities of the resulting outcomes. (We may call this number the expected utility of the action.) As I do not know what outcome, and thus what utility, will be associated with the action that I choose we can no longer consider my choice to be rational on the basis of its resulting utility. We may, however, consider my choice to be rational if, for some way of assigning utilities to outcomes, the action which I choose is that with the highest expected utility. In Chapter 2 we characterise the choices which are rational in this wider sense; and in Chapter 3 we discuss the attitudes to risk which are embodied in such choices.

Thus far we have assumed that Nature, in choosing the environment, is either dormant, as when outcomes are certain, or blind, as when they are uncertain. We now allow Nature to have her own agenda. We assume that Nature is rational and thus associates her own utilities with outcomes. Nontrivial choices are now made both by me and by Nature. If I knew the probability with which Nature chose each environment then I could make a rational response to these probabilities, namely, that with the highest expected utility. In fact, I do not know these probabilities, but I may infer something about them. Specifically, I may infer that each environment which I consider Nature might choose (that is, each environment with a positive probability) will be a rational response to the probabilities with which I choose my actions. Further, as Nature is rational, I should anticipate that Nature makes an analogous inference. Indeed, I should anticipate that Nature anticipates that I make an analogous inference, and so forth ad infinitum. We consider my and Nature's choices to be rational if they arise from our each following this chain of reasoning. In Chapter 4 we characterise the choices, for me and for Nature, which are rational in this extended sense; and in Chapter 5 we discuss the concept of knowledge and its relation to such rationality.

Chapters 1, 2 and 4 develop frameworks for discussing rational choice with increasing generality. (Chapters 3 and 5 are digressions on Chapters 2 and 4, respectively.) The parameters of the most general problem are:

(a) a set of actions from which I choose;

(b) a set of environments from which Nature chooses;

(c) a set of outcomes;

(d) a rule associating an outcome with each action in each environment; and

(e) a specification of Nature's preferences over outcomes.

This general problem is the problem of strategic choice. The problem of choice under uncertainty is the special case of the general problem in which Nature is indifferent between all outcomes and thus chooses randomly. And the problem of pure choice is the special case of the general problem in which there is only one environment. We draw on the characterisation of rationality in the problem of pure choice to characterise rationality in the context of choice under uncertainty, and draw on this characterisation to characterise rationality in the context of strategic choice.

An alternative generalisation of the problem of pure choice is that of social choice. There are now a number of individuals, each of whom makes rational choices in the sense developed in Chapter 1. A social choice rule specifies both the choices that are made by society and the way in which these take account of the preferences of the individuals in society. Such a rule is admissible if it takes account of individual preferences in some consistent way; it is rational if the choices which it makes are rational, again in the sense developed in Chapter 1. In Chapter 6 we characterise the admissible choice rules which are rational.

The relationships between the four problems outlined above are illustrated in Figure 0.1.

The formal treatment of all four problems originates in the middle of the twentieth century: that of pure choice with Samuelson's *Foundations* (1947); that of choice under uncertainty with von Neumann and Morgenstern's *Theory of Games* (1944); that of strategic choice with Nash's *Annals of Mathematics* article (1951); and that of social choice with Arrow's *Social Choice and Individual Values* (1951).

The approach is axiomatic. Debreu, in his Nobel Laureate address, defines such an approach as one 'in which primitive concepts are chosen, assumptions concerning them are

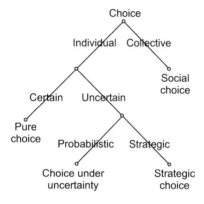

Figure 0.1

formulated, and conclusions are derived from those assumptions by means of mathematical reasoning disconnected from any intended interpretation of primitive concepts' (1984, p. 275). Or, as Hilbert is reported, in Reid's *Life*, to have said, 'one must be able to say at all times – instead of points, straight lines, and planes – tables, chairs and beer mugs' (1970, p. 54). In short, theory is divorced from interpretation.

In this book the theory is contained solely in the definitions, propositions, proofs and remarks (that is, self-evident propositions). The interpretation of this theory, which gives it its relevance, is contained in the remainder of the text. Illustrations of the theory are presented in a number of examples. In some cases, usually indicated by the phrase 'as may be verified', these also act as exercises: in such cases the argument is only sketched and should completed by the reader.

Although the treatment is abstract, technicalities are kept to a minimum. The only mathematics which is used is that of simple operations on finite sets and on the rational numbers. No recourse is made to the real numbers or to mathematical analysis. An outline of all the set and number theory which is

used in the book is presented in the Appendix. The reader
who is not familiar with sets and numbers should read this
appendix before proceeding to Chapter 1.

References, connections with related topics and sources for
axioms and results which are neither well known nor original
to this book are given in the notes at the end of each chapter.

Choice is pervasive in life, and living and faring well means
choosing well. Although an understanding of the logic of
rational choice is a worthwhile end in itself it is also the
central component of eudaimonia.

1 Choice

We address the problem of pure choice. We first set out the problem, propose a definition of a basic consistency requirement, that of reasonableness, and characterise the set of choice rules which are reasonable. We then define a stronger requirement, that of rationality, and characterise the choice rules which are rational. We conclude with a discussion of the relation between choice and utility.

CHOICE PROBLEMS

The objects between which choice is made, or outcomes, are taken as primitive: loosely speaking, an outcome is anything that may happen. To avoid trivialities we assume throughout that there are as many outcomes as may be needed for the argument in hand.

We also assume that the set X of all potentially available outcomes is finite. This assumption excludes the possibility of the set being dense but bounded, as is the set of times in some given day or as is the unit interval $\mathbb{I}$. It also excludes its being unbounded, as is the set of all future days or as is the set $\mathbb{N}$ of natural numbers. In the first case it may be possible to approximate the set of outcomes by a finite set. For example, $\mathbb{I}$ may be approximated as closely as desired by the finite set

$$\{1/n, \ 2/n, \ldots, (n-1)/n\}$$

simply by making the natural number n sufficiently large. Such approximation is not possible in the second case: $\mathbb{N}$ cannot be approximated by any finite set. In this second case choice may be impossible: it is not possible to choose the highest natural number. However, most interesting choice problems are bounded.

A choice problem is defined by a nonempty set of available outcomes: the empty set is excluded as the question of choice does not arise if there is nothing from which to choose.

Definition. A choice problem is specified by a nonempty subset of some fixed finite set X. ∎

We are concerned with choosing one or more outcomes from various sets of available outcomes: that is, from various subsets of X. Any outcome which is chosen must be available or choice would be meaningless. And some outcome must be chosen as not choosing does not constitute choice. However, multiple outcomes may be chosen as there may be no reason for choosing one outcome over another. Note that the sole outcome chosen from a singleton set must, trivially, be the outcome in the set.

A choice rule associates a set of chosen outcomes with each choice problem.

Definition. A choice rule on the family of choice problems (or for X) is a function C taking each nonempty $S \subset X$ to some nonempty $C(S) \subset S$. ∎

Example 1.1. Let

$$X = \{x, y, z\}$$

and C be specified by

$$C(X) = \{x, y\}, \ C(\{x, y\}) = \{x, y\},$$
$$C(\{y, z\}) = \{y\}, \ C(\{x, z\}) = \{x\}$$

(with $C(S) = S$ for each singleton $S \subset X$). Then C is a choice rule for X. ∎

Consider a relation $\succeq$ on the set X, the symmetric and asymmetric components of which are $\sim$ and $\succ$. The maximal subset of a set S of outcomes with respect to $\succeq$ is the set of outcomes which stand in the relation $\succeq$ to all other outcomes in S. Equivalently, it is the set of outcomes x which are undominated in S: that is, for which there is no outcome y in S such that $y \succ x$.

Definition. The maximal subset $M(S. \succeq)$ of $S \subset X$ with respect to the relation $\succeq$ on X is

$$\{x \in S : x \succeq y \text{ for all } y \in S\}. \blacksquare$$

Example 1.2. Let

$$X = \{x, y, z\}$$

and $\succeq$ be specified by

$$x \sim y, \ y \succ z, \ x \succ z.$$

Then

$$M(X, \succeq) = \{x, y\}, M(\{x, y\}, \succeq) = \{x, y\},$$
$$M(\{y, z\}, \succeq) = \{y\}, M(\{x, z\}, \succeq) = \{x\}$$

(and $M(S, \succeq) = S$ for each singleton $S \subset X$). $\blacksquare$

REASONABLE CHOICE

We consider a choice rule to be reasonable if there is a relation $\succeq$ on the set X of outcomes such that the set of outcomes chosen from any subset S of X is the maximal subset of S with respect to $\succeq$. If this obtains then we may interpret $\succeq$ as 'is at least as good as', $\sim$ as 'is indifferent to' and $\succ$ as 'is better than'. Then choice is reasonable if the outcomes that are chosen are those which are at least as good as all other outcomes. In this case we consider the relation 'at least as good as' to be a reason for the choice rule.

Definition. The choice rule C for X is reasonable if, for all $S \subset X$, $C(S)$ is the maximal subset of S with respect to some relation $\succeq$ on X; if this obtains then $\succeq$ is a reason for C. ∎

Example 1.3. Let X and C be specified as in Example 1.1 and $\succeq$ be specified as in Example 1.2. Then $\succeq$ is a reason for C. ∎

The following proposition shows that a reason must be both complete and acyclic and thus a quasi-ordering.

Proposition. If a choice rule C for X is reasonable then its reason $\succeq$ is a quasi-ordering. ∎

Proof. Let

$$S = \{x, y\} \subset X.$$

If not $x \succeq y$ and not $y \succeq x$ then $M(S, \succeq)$ is empty which is inconsistent with

$$C(S) = M(S, \succeq)$$

as $C(S)$ is nonempty. Thus $\succeq$ is complete. Let

$$T = \{x, y, z\} \subset X.$$

If

$$x \succ y, \ y \succ z, \ z \succ x$$

then $M(T, \succeq)$ is empty which is inconsistent with

$$C(T) = M(T, \succeq)$$

as $C(T)$ is nonempty. Thus $\succeq$ is acyclic. It follows that $\succeq$ is a quasi-ordering. ∎

A natural candidate for a reason for a choice rule is its base relation. This specifies that an outcome x is at least as good as a second outcome y if x is chosen out of x and y, irrespective of whether y is also chosen.

Definition. The base relation $\succeq$ for the choice rule C for X is defined by $x \succeq y$ if and only if

$$x \in C(\{x, y\})$$

for some $x, y \in X$. ∎

Example 1.4. Let X and C be specified as in Example 1.1 and $\succeq$ be specified as in Example 1.2. Then $\succeq$ is the base relation for C. ∎

The following proposition shows that if a choice rule has a reason then this must be its base relation.

Proposition. If a choice rule C for X is reasonable then its unique reason is its base relation $\succeq$. ∎

Proof. Let C be reasonable and $\succeq'$ be a reason for C. Then, for all $x, y \in X$, $x \succeq y$ if and only if

$$x \in C(\{x, y\})$$

which obtains if and only if

$$x \in M(\{x, y\}, \succeq')$$

which obtains if and only if $x \succeq' y$. Thus $\succeq' = \succeq$. ∎

Not all choice rules are reasonable, as the following two examples show.

Example 1.5. Let

$$X = \{x, y, z\}$$

and C be specified by

$$C(X) = \{x\}, \ C(\{x, y\}) = \{x\},$$
$$C(\{y, z\}) = \{z\}, \ C(\{x, z\}) = \{x, z\}.$$

If $\succeq$ is a reason for C then $x \succ z$ as $C(X) = \{x\}$, and $x \sim z$ as

$$C(\{x, z\}) = \{x, z\}.$$

It follows from this contradiction that C is not reasonable. For future reference note that $C(X) = \{x\}$ and that, for all $S \subset X$, if $x \in S$ then $x \in C(S)$. ∎

Example 1.6. Let

$$X = \{x, y, z\}$$

and C be specified by

$$C(X) = \{x\}, \ C(\{x, y\}) = \{y\},$$
$$C(\{y, z\}) = \{z\}, \ C(\{x, z\}) = \{x\}.$$

If $\succeq$ is a reason for C then $x \succeq y$ as $C(X) = \{x\}$, and $y \succ x$ as

$$C(\{x, y\}) = \{y\}.$$

It follows from this contradiction that C is not reasonable. For future reference note that there is no outcome which is chosen when paired with each other outcome. ∎

THE EXPANSION AND CONTRACTION AXIOMS

The problem in Example 1.5 is that the outcome z is chosen both out of x and z and out of y and z but is not chosen out of x, y and z. To avoid such problems we require that if some outcome is chosen when it is paired with every other outcome in a set then this outcome is chosen from the set. This requirement is the expansion axiom (also known as the condorcet axiom).

Definition. The choice rule C for X satisfies the expansion axiom if, for all $S \subset X$, the conditions $x \in S$ and

$$x \in C(\{x, y\})$$

for all $y \in S$ imply that $x \in C(S)$. ■

The problem in Example 1.6 is that the outcome x is chosen out of x, y and z but is not chosen out of x and y. To avoid such problems we require that if an outcome is chosen from some set and remains available in some subset of this set then it is chosen from this subset. This requirement is the contraction axiom (also known as Chernoff's axiom and as Sen's alpha property).

Definition. The choice rule C for X satisfies the contraction axiom if, for all S, $T \subset X$, the conditions $x \in S \subset T$ and $x \in C(T)$ imply that $x \in C(S)$. ■

An explanation of the contraction axiom (when referred to as Sen's alpha property, and then in the words of its author) is that 'if the world champion of some game is a Pakistani then he must be the champion in Pakistan' (although, to be more precise, each occurrence of 'the' should be replaced by 'a'). An analogous explanation of the expansion axiom is that if some Pakistani is not defeated by any other Pakistani then he must be a champion in Pakistan.

The following remark is obtained by substituting $C(S)$ for S and S for T in the definition of the contraction axiom.

Remark. If a choice rule C for X satisfies the contraction axiom then

$$C(C(S)) = C(S)$$

for all $S \subset X$. ■

This remark supports our permitting more than one outcome to be chosen from a set of available outcomes. If more than one outcome is chosen then there can be no basis for choosing any particular one: that is, the set of chosen outcomes cannot be reduced by choosing again.

The expansion and contraction axioms are independent: that is, the satisfaction of the first axiom implies neither the satisfaction nor the failure of the second, and the satisfaction of the second implies neither the satisfaction nor the failure of the first. Equivalently, there exist choice rules which satisfy both axioms, rules which satisfy precisely one axiom, and rules which satisfy neither axiom. The choice rule in Example 1.5 satisfies the contraction axiom, as the observation for future reference made in this example shows, but clearly fails to satisfy the expansion axiom; and the choice rule in Example 1.6 satisfies the expansion axiom, again as the observation for future reference shows, but clearly fails to satisfy the contraction axiom. Examples of choice rules which satisfy both axioms and of those which satisfy neither are obvious.

The following two propositions show that the expansion and contraction axioms together are necessary and sufficient for a choice rule to be reasonable. We thus have a complete characterisation of the set of reasonable choice rules.

Proposition. If choice rule C for X is reasonable then it satisfies the expansion and contraction axioms. ∎

Proof. Let $\succeq$ be the reason for C. Assume that $x \in S \subset X$ and

$$x \in C(\{x, y\})$$

for all $y \in S$. Then $x \succeq y$ for all $y \in S$ so that $x \in C(S)$. Thus C satisfies the expansion axiom. Now assume that

$$x \in S \subset T \subset X$$

and $x \in C(T)$ but $x \notin C(S)$. Then there is some $y \in S \subset T$ such that $y \succ x$ so that $x \notin C(T)$. It follows from this contradiction that C satisfies the contraction axiom. ∎

Proposition. If a choice rule C for X satisfies the expansion and contraction axioms then it is reasonable. ∎

Proof. Let $\succeq$ be the base relation for C, $y \in T \subset X$ and $x \in C(T)$. Then $\{x, y\} \subset T$ so, by the contraction axiom,

$$x \in C(\{x, y\}).$$

and $x \succeq y$. Thus $x \in M(T, \succeq)$ so that

$$C(T) \subset M(T, \succeq).$$

Now if $v \in M(T, \succeq)$ then, for all $w \in T$, $v \succeq w$ and thus

$$v \in C(\{v, w\}),$$

Then, by the expansion axiom, $v \in C(T)$ so that

$$M(T, \succeq) \subset C(T).$$

It follows that

$$C(T) = M(T, \succeq)$$

so that C is reasonable. ∎

RATIONAL CHOICE

Not all reasons can properly be considered to be to be rational. In particular, the concept of 'at least as good as' could not be considered to be rational if an outcome x were at least as good as a second outcome y and y were at least as good as a third outcome z but x were not at least as good as z. The problem with this reason is that it is intransitive: the concept of transitivity may be seen as being embedded in that of rationality. Accordingly, we consider a choice rule to be rational if it has a transitive reason or, equivalently, if it has a reason which is an ordering.

Definition. A choice rule C for X is rational if it has a transitive reason. ■

The following example shows that the extension from reasonableness to rationality is nontrivial: that is, although the reason for a choice rule must be a quasi-ordering it may not be an ordering.

Example 1.7. Let

$$X = \{x, y, z\}$$

and C be specified by

$$C(X) = \{x\}, \ C(\{x, y\}) = \{x, y\},$$

$$C(\{y, z\}) = \{z\}, \ C(\{x, z\}) = \{x\}.$$

The relation $\succeq$ specified by

$$x \sim y, \ z \succ y, \ x \succ z$$

is a reason for C so that C is reasonable. However, $\succeq$ is not transitive so that C is not rational. For future reference note that

$$x \in \{x, y\} \cap C(X)$$

but

$$\{x, y\} \cap C(X) \neq C(\{x, y\}). \ ■$$

THE CONGRUENCE AXIOM

The problem in Example 1.7 is that both outcomes x and y are chosen out of x and y but only x is chosen out of x, y and z. The contraction axiom requires that if some outcome in the smaller set is chosen from the larger then this outcome is chosen from the smaller. The problem in Example 1.7 arises because the reverse implication is not satisfied. To avoid this problem we require that all and only those outcomes chosen from a set which are contained in some subset of this set, if there are any, are chosen from this subset. This requirement is the congruence axiom (also known as Arrow's axiom).

Definition. A choice rule C for X satisfies the congruence axiom if, for all S, $T \subset X$, the condition $S \subset T$ implies that either

$$C(S) = S \cap C(T)$$

or $S \cap C(T)$ is empty. ∎

An explanation of this axiom on lines analogous to the explanations of the expansion and contraction axioms is that if any Pakistani is a world champion then every Pakistani who is a world champion is a champion in Pakistan and every champion in Pakistan is a world champion.

It is apparent that the congruence axiom implies the contraction axiom. The following proposition confirms this and also shows that the congruence axiom implies the expansion axiom.

Proposition. If a choice rule C for X satisfies the congruence axiom then it satisfies the expansion and contraction axioms. ∎

Proof. Let $\succeq$ be the base relation for C, $T \subset X$, $x \in M(T, \succeq)$ and $y \in C(T)$. Then $y \in T$ so that $x \succeq y$. As $\{x, y\} \subset T$ and

$$\{x, y\} \cap C(T)$$

is nonempty the congruence axiom implies that

$$\{x, y\} \cap C(T) = C(\{x, y\}).$$

As

$$x \in C(\{x, y\})$$

it follows that $x \in C(T)$ so that

$$M(T, \succeq) \subset C(T).$$

Thus if $v \in T$ and

$$v \in C(\{v, w\})$$

for all $w \in T$ then $v \in C(T)$ so that the expansion axiom is satisfied. Now let $z \in S \subset T$ and $z \in C(T)$. Then

$$z \in S \cap C(T) = C(S)$$

by the congruence axiom so that the contraction axiom is satisfied. ∎

The converse of this proposition is false: as the choice rule of Example 1.7 is reasonable it satisfies the expansion and contraction axioms but, as the observation for future reference made in this example shows, it fails to satisfy the congruence axiom. Thus the congruence axiom is stronger than the expansion and contraction axioms together.

The following two propositions show that the congruence axiom is both necessary and sufficient for a choice rule to be rational. We thus have a first complete characterisation of the set of rational choice rules.

Proposition. If a choice rule C for X is rational then it satisfies the congruence axiom. ■

Proof. Let $\succeq$ be the reason for C and let $S \subset T \subset X$ with $S \cap C(T)$ nonempty. As C is reasonable the contraction axiom is satisfied and thus

$$S \cap C(T) \subset C(S).$$

Now let $z \in C(S)$ so that $z \succeq v$ for all $v \in S$. If $z \notin C(T)$ then there is some $w \in T$ such that $w \succ z$. Let $v \in S \cap C(T)$ so that $v \succeq w$. Then, as $\succeq$ is transitive, $v \succ z$ which contradicts $z \in C(S)$ and $v \in S$. Thus $z \in C(T)$ so that

$$C(S) \subset S \cap C(T).$$

It follows that

$$S \cap C(T) = C(S)$$

so that the congruence axiom is satisfied. ■

Proposition. If a choice rule C for X satisfies the congruence axiom then it is rational. ■

Proof. As C satisfies the congruence axiom it has a reason; let this be $\succeq$. Let $x, y, z \in X$ with $x \succeq y$ and $y \succeq z$ and let

$$T = \{x, y, z\}.$$

First assume that $x \notin C(T)$. If $y \in C(T)$ then, by the congruence axiom,

$$\{y\} = \{x, y\} \cap C(T) = C(\{x, y\})$$

which contradicts $x \succeq y$. Thus $x \notin C(T)$ implies that $y \notin C(T)$. Next, assume that $y \notin C(T)$. If $z \in C(T)$ then, by the congruence axiom,

$$\{z\} = \{y,z\} \cap C(T) = C(\{y,z\})$$

which contradicts $y \succeq z$. Thus $y \notin C(T)$ implies that $z \notin C(T)$. As $C(T)$ is nonempty it follows that $x \in C(T)$. Then

$$x \in \{x,z\} \cap C(T) = C(\{x,z\}).$$

It follows that $x \succeq z$ so that $\succeq$ is transitive and C is rational. ∎

PREFERENCE REVELATION

We have characterised the set of rational choice rules using the congruence axiom as this is an immediate strengthening of the contraction axiom as well as a strengthening of the expansion axiom, which axioms together provide a necessary and sufficient condition for a choice rule to be reasonable.

An equivalent characterisation uses the concept of preference revelation. This requires that if an outcome x is ever chosen when another outcome y is available (that is, if x is revealed preferred to y) then whenever y is chosen and x is available x is also chosen (that is, y is not revealed preferred to x). This requirement is the revealed preference axiom (also known as Houthakker's axiom).

Definition. A choice rule C for X satisfies the revealed preference axiom if, for all $S, T \subset X$, the conditions $x, y \in S \cap T, x \in C(S)$ and $y \in C(T)$ imply that $y \in C(S)$ and $x \in C(T)$. ∎

An explanation of this axiom on lines analogous to the explanations of the preceding axioms is that if there are two Pakistani men and one is a (world) men's champion and the other a (unisex) Pakistani champion then the first is also a Pakistani champion and the second is also a men's champion. If this appears implausible note that the men's champion cannot be defeated by the Pakistani champion as the latter is a man, and the Pakistani champion cannot be defeated by the world champion as the latter is a Pakistani. Thus if the two meet, which is to say if the relation 'is not defeated by' is complete, then they must tie. This implies that each must be both a men's champion and a Pakistani champion.

The following proposition shows that the revealed preference axiom is equivalent to the congruence axiom.

Proposition. A choice rule C for X satisfies the revealed preference axiom if and only if it satisfies the congruence axiom. ∎

Proof. First, assume that C satisfies the congruence axiom. Let $S, T \subset X$ and assume that $x, y \in S \cap T$ with $x \in C(S)$ and $y \in C(T)$. As $S \cap T \subset S$ and $S \cap T \subset T$

$$(S \cap T) \cap C(S) = C(S \cap T) = (S \cap T) \cap C(T)$$

by the congruence axiom. Then $x \in C(T)$ and $y \in C(S)$ so that the revealed preference axiom is satisfied. To prove the converse, let $S \subset T \subset X$ with

$$x \in C(S) \subset S \cap T.$$

If $S \cap C(T)$ is empty then the congruence axiom is satisfied immediately. Assume, then, that

$$y \in S \cap C(T) \subset S \cap T.$$

Then $y \in C(T)$ so, by the revealed preference axiom, $y \in C(S)$ so that

$$S \cap C(T) \subset C(S).$$

Also by the revealed preference axiom,

$$x \in C(T) \subset S \cap C(T)$$

so that

$$C(S) \subset S \cap C(T).$$

It follows that

$$S \cap C(T) = C(S)$$

so that the congruence axiom is satisfied. ■

The remark below follows from this proposition and from the equivalence between the congruence axiom and rationality. It provides a second characterisation of the set of rational choice rules.

Remark. A choice rule is rational if and only if it satisfies the revealed preference axiom. ■

THE EXTENSION AXIOM

Yet another characterisation of the set of rational choice rules uses the contraction axiom and an alternative to the expansion axiom. The latter is the extension axiom (also known as Sen's beta property). This requires that if the outcomes x and y are both chosen from a set S and x is chosen from a set which contains S then y is also chosen from this containing set. An explanation of this property given by its author is that 'if some Pakistani is a world champion then all champions of Pakistan must be champions of the world'.

Definition. A choice rule C for X satisfies the extension axiom if, for all S, $T \subset X$, the conditions $S \subset T$, $x \in C(T)$ and x, $y \in C(S)$ imply that $y \in C(T)$. ■

The expansion and extension axioms, although concerned with similar situations, are independent. The choice rules in the following two examples satisfy precisely one of these axioms; examples of choice rules which satisfy both axioms and of those which satisfy neither are obvious. (However, if the contraction axiom is satisfied then the extension axiom implies the expansion axiom, as is shown later.)

Example 1.8. Let

$$X = \{x, y, z\}$$

and C be specified by

$$C(X) = \{y, z\}, C(\{x, y\}) = \{x\},$$
$$C(\{y, z\}) = \{y, z\}, C(\{x, z\}) = \{x\}.$$

Then

$$C(\{y, z\}) = \{y, z\} = C(X)$$

and $C(S)$ is singleton for all proper subsets of X other than $\{y, z\}$ so that C satisfies the extension axiom. However,

$$x \in C(\{x, y\})$$

and

$$x \in C(\{x, z\})$$

but $x \notin C(X)$ so that C does not satisfy the expansion axiom. ■

Example 1.9. Let

$$X = \{x, y, z\}$$

and C be specified by

$$C(X) = \{x\}, C(\{x, y\}) = \{x\},$$
$$C(\{y, z\}) = \{y\}, C(\{x, z\}) = \{x, z\}.$$

Then x is the only outcome which is chosen when paired with each other outcome and $x \in C(X)$ so that C satisfies the expansion axiom. However,

$$x, z \in C(\{x, z\})$$

and $x \in C(X)$ but $z \notin C(X)$ so that C does not satisfy the extension axiom. ∎

The following two propositions show that the extension and contraction axioms together are necessary and sufficient for a choice rule to be rational. We thus have a third characterisation of the set of rational choice rules.

Proposition. If a choice rule C for X is rational then it satisfies the extension and contraction axioms. ∎

Proof. Let $\succeq$ be the reason for C. If $x \in S \subset T$ and $x \in C(T)$ then $x \succeq y$ for all $y \in T$ so that $x \succeq y$ for all $y \in S$ and $x \in C(S)$. Thus the contraction axiom is satisfied. Now let v, $w \in C(S)$ and $v \in C(T)$. Then $w \succeq v$ and $v \succeq z$ for all $z \in T$ so that, as $\succeq$ is transitive, $w \succeq z$ for all $z \in T$. Thus $w \in C(T)$ and the extension axiom is satisfied. ∎

Proposition. If a choice rule C for X satisfies the extension and contraction axioms then it is rational. ∎

Proof. Let $\succeq$ be the base relation for C, $y \in S \subset X$ and $x \in C(S)$. As $\{x, y\} \subset S$

$$x \in C(\{x, y\}),$$

by the contraction axiom, so that $x \succeq y$ and $x \in M(S, \succeq)$. Thus

$$C(S) \subset M(S, \succeq).$$

Now assume that $y \notin C(S)$ and let $z \in C(S)$. Then, as $\{y, z\} \subset S$,

$$C(\{y,z\}) = \{z\},$$

by the extension and contraction axioms. Thus $z \succ y$ so that $y \notin M(S, \succeq)$. Hence

$$M(S, \succeq) \subset C(S).$$

It follows that

$$C(S) = M(S, \succeq)$$

so that $\succeq$ is a reason for C. To show that $\succeq$ is transitive assume that $u \succeq v$ and $v \succeq w$ and suppose that $w \succ u$. Then

$$u \notin C(\{u, w\})$$

so that

$$u \notin C(\{u, v, w\}),$$

by the contraction axiom. As

$$u \in C(\{u, v\})$$

this implies that

$$v \notin C(\{u, v, w\}),$$

by the extension axiom, so that, as

$$v \in C(\{v, w\}),$$

the extension axiom implies that

$$w \notin C(\{u, v, w\}).$$

Thus $C(\{u, v, w\})$ is empty. It follows from this contradiction that $u \succeq w$ so that $\succeq$ is transitive and C is rational. ∎

Since the extension and contraction axioms imply rationality which in turn implies reasonableness which in turn implies the expansion axiom, it follows (as claimed earlier) that in the presence of the contraction axiom the extension axiom implies the expansion axiom.

Remark. If a choice rule C satisfies the contraction axiom and the extension axiom then it satisfies the expansion axiom. ∎

However, even in the presence of the contraction axiom the expansion axiom does not imply the extension axiom since, given the contraction axiom, the former is equivalent to reasonableness and the latter to rationality, and reasonableness does not imply rationality.

UTILITY

A utility representation for a relation $\succeq$ on the set of outcomes is a way of assigning rational numbers to outcomes or, equivalently, a function from the set X of outcomes to $\mathbb{Q}$, such that the number assigned to an outcome x is at least as great as that assigned to another outcome y if and only if $x \succeq y$. The number assigned to an outcome is the utility of that outcome and 'is at least as good as' has the same meaning as 'has at least as great a utility as'. It is clear that if u is a utility representation for $\succeq$ then so is any increasing transformation of u: that is, any composite function fu where f is a function from $\mathbb{Q}$ to $\mathbb{Q}$ with the property that if $a > b$ then $f(a) > f(b)$.

Definition. A utility representation u for a relation $\succeq$ on X is a function from X to $\mathbb{Q}$ such that, for all $x, y \in X$, $u(x) \geq u(y)$ if and only if $x \succeq y$. ∎

Example 1.10. Let

$$X = \{x, y, z\}$$

and $\succeq$ be specified as in Example 1.2. Then the function u defined by

$$u(x) = 1, \ u(y) = 1, \ u(z) = 0$$

and the function v defined by

$$v(x) = 2, \ v(y) = 2, \ v(z) = 0$$

are each utility representations for $\succeq$. ∎

The following proposition shows that a necessary and sufficient condition for a relation to have a utility representation is that it is an ordering.

Proposition. A relation $\succeq$ on X has a utility representation u if and only if it is an ordering. ∎

Proof. First, assume that u is a utility representation for $\succeq$ and let $x, y, z \in X$. Then either $u(x) \geq u(y)$ or $u(y) \geq u(x)$ so that either $x \succeq y$ or $y \succeq x$; thus $\succeq$ is complete. Now assume that $x \succeq y$ and $y \succeq z$. Then $u(x) \geq u(y)$ and $u(y) \geq u(z)$ so that $u(x) \geq u(z)$; thus $x \succeq z$ and $\succeq$ is transitive. It follows that u is an ordering. To prove the converse, define the function u from x to $\mathbb{Q}$ by $u(x) = \#W(x)$ where

$$W(x) = \{y \in X : x \succeq y\}.$$

Assume that $x \sim z$: then $x \succeq y$ if and only if $z \succeq y$ so that $W(x) = W(z)$ and thus $u(x) = u(z)$. Alternatively, assume that $x \succ z$: then $x \succeq y$ if $z \succeq y$ so that $W(z) \subset W(x)$; but

$$x \in W(x) \setminus W(z)$$

so that $W(z) \neq W(x)$ and $u(x) > u(z)$. It follows that $u(x) \geq u(y)$ if and only if $x \succeq y$ so that u is a utility representation for $\succeq$. ∎

We define a choice rule to have a utility representation if its reason has one.

Definition   A choice rule for X has a utility representation if it has a reason which has a utility representation. ■

The remark below follows from this definition, the preceding proposition and the definition of rationality.

Remark. A choice rule for X is rational if and only if it has a utility representation. ■

AN OVERVIEW

The relationships between reasonableness, rationality, utility and the various axioms proposed above are illustrated in Figure 1.1.

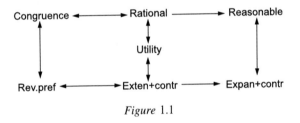

Figure 1.1

Notes

Outcomes are interpreted in the same sense as are Savage's consequences: that is, as 'anything which may happen' (1954, p. 13). The concept of a base relation for a choice rule is due to Arrow (1959) and Herzberger (1973). The embedded nature of transitivity is developed by Arrow: 'the idea of transitivity clearly corresponds to some strong feeling of the meaning of consistency in our choice' (1967, p. 5). The extension that choosing rationally means maximising utility is analysed further by Sen (1997).

The contraction, expansion, congruence and revealed preference axioms are due to Blair, Bordes, Kelly and Suzumura (1976), Chernoff (1954), Arrow (1959) and Houthakker (1950), respectively. Sen's alpha and beta properties are due to Sen (1969, p. 384).

A survey of the relation between choice rules and their reasons is provided by Suzumura (1983) and that of the relation between reasons and their utility representations by Fishburn (1970).

2 Uncertainty

We address the problem of choice under uncertainty as a generalisation of the problem of pure choice. We start with the case where there are some given objective probabilities: we set out the problem, propose a definition of rationality and provide a characterisation of the choice rules which are rational. We then extend the discussion, less formally, to the case where such probabilities are not given.

UNCERTAINTY PROBLEMS

The problem addressed in Chapter 1 was that of choosing an outcome: my choice over outcomes is rational if the outcomes that I choose are those with the highest utility. An alternative interpretation of this problem is that instead of my being given a set of outcomes I am given a set of acts and a rule which associates some unique outcome with each act. In this interpretation my choice over acts is rational if the acts that I choose are those whose associated outcomes have the highest utility.

We now turn to the more general problem of my choosing an act the result of which depends on some event that occurs by chance as well as on this act. An event is a description of some aspect of the physical universe: for example, one event may be that a coin displays heads and another that it displays tails. Events are defined in such a way that precisely one must occur. I am now given a finite set A of acts over which I choose, a finite set T of events and a rule f which specifies the outcome $f(a, t)$ which obtains if I choose the act a and the event t occurs.

I do not know what event will occur but I do know the probability $m(t)$ of the event t occurring: that is, I am given a probability distribution m on the set T.

Let $F(a, x)$ denote the (possibly empty) set of events which together with the act a result in the outcome x; that is, let

$$F(a,x) = \{t \in T : f(a,t) = x\}.$$

Then if I choose the act a the probability of my achieving the outcome x is

$$\sum [t \in F(a,x)]\, m(t)$$

(if the set $F(a,x)$ is empty this probability is 0). This means that choosing an act a is equivalent to choosing the probability distribution $p(.\,;\,a)$ on the set X of outcomes defined by

$$p(x;a) = \sum [t \in F(a,x)]\, m(t).$$

For example, if all events are equiprobable then

$$p(x;a) = \#F(a,x)/\#T.$$

We may then interpret the problem of choice under uncertainty as being that of choosing over a set of probability distributions on X; we refer to such probability distributions as lotteries.

Not all lotteries are available. As there cannot be more available lotteries than there are acts, and as the set of acts is finite, there is only a finite number of available lotteries. To avoid trivialities we assume throughout that there are as many available lotteries as may be needed for the argument in hand.

Example 2.1. Let

$$A = \{a,b\}, T = \{s,t\}, X = \{x,y,z\},$$

f be specified by

$$f(a,s) = x,\ f(a,t) = y,$$
$$f(b,s) = z,\ f(b,t) = z$$

and s and t be equiprobable. Then if a is chosen x or y is obtained, each with probability $1/2$; and if b is chosen z is obtained with probability 1. Thus the available lotteries are p and q such that

$$p(x) = p(y) = 1/2$$

and $q(z) = 1$. ∎

An uncertainty problem is defined by a specified set of lotteries. Note that a pure choice problem is the special case of an uncertainty problem in which there is only one state.

Definition. An uncertainty problem is specified by the pair (Q,X) where Q is a nonempty finite subset of the set of probability distributions on some fixed finite set X. ∎

A choice rule in the present context associates a set of chosen lotteries with each uncertainty problem.

Definition. A choice rule on the family of uncertainty problems is a function taking (Q,X) to some nonempty $C \subset Q$. ∎

RATIONALITY AND EXPECTED UTILITY

Choice over the set of probability distributions on a set of outcomes is rational if, first, it reflects rational preferences on the set of outcomes and, second, it takes rational account of the relevant probabilities. As was established in Chapter 1, the first of these requirements implies that there is a utility function defined on the set of outcomes such that chosen outcomes maximise utility. We interpret the second requirement as being that this utility function is such that chosen probability distributions maximise expected utility: that is, the sum of the utility of each outcome weighted by the probability of its occurring. More formally, choice over the set of lotteries is rational if there is some utility function *u* defined on the set of outcomes such that chosen lotteries maximise

$$\sum [x \in X] \, p(x) \cdot u(x),$$

which sum we now write more simply as $\sum p(x) \cdot u(x)$, over *p* in *P*.

Definition. The choice rule taking (Q, X) to *C* is rational if there is a function *u* from *X* to $\mathbb{Q}$ such that $p \in C$ if and only if

$$\sum p(x) \cdot u(x) \geq \sum q(x) \cdot u(x)$$

for all $q \in Q$. ∎

As was established in Chapter 1, a necessary condition for a choice rule on any set, including the set of lotteries, to be rational is that it has a transitive reason: that is, that there is an ordering $\succeq$ on the set such that chosen elements are maximal with respect to $\succeq$. Rationality in the present context requires that the maximal elements with respect to $\succeq$ are those which maximise the expected value of some utility function defined on the set of outcomes. If this obtains then the ordering $\succeq$ is said to have the expected utility property, and the utility function which it invokes is said to be a cardinal utility function.

Definition. The ordering $\succeq$ on the set *P* of probability distributions on *X* has the expected utility property if there is a function *u* from *X* to $\mathbb{Q}$ such that, for all $p, q \in P$, $p \succeq q$ if and only if

$$\sum p(x) \cdot u(x) \geq \sum q(x) \cdot u(x);$$

if this obtains then *u* is a cardinal utility function for $\succeq$. ∎

Characterising the set of rational choice rules is then equivalent to characterising the set of orderings which have the expected utility property, as the following remark notes.

Remark. The choice rule taking (Q, X) to C is rational if and only if it has a reason with the expected utility property: that is, if and only if

$$C = \{p \in Q : p \succeq q \text{ for all } q \in Q\}.$$

for some ordering $\succeq$ on the set of probability distributions on X with the expected utility property. ∎

A cardinal utility function, on which the expected utility property rests, is not unique: the following proposition shows that any affine transformation preserves the expected utility property. (A function v from X to $\mathbb{Q}$ is an affine transformation of u if $f = a + b \cdot u$ for some a in $\mathbb{Q}$ and b in $\mathbb{Q} \setminus \{0\}$.)

Proposition. If u is a cardinal utility function for an ordering $\succeq$ on P then, for all a in $\mathbb{Q}$ and b in $\mathbb{Q} \setminus \{0\}$, $v = a + b \cdot u$ is a cardinal utility function for $\succeq$. ∎

Proof. Define the functions f and g from P to $\mathbb{Q}$ by

$$f(p) = \sum p(x) \cdot u(x)$$

and

$$g(p) = \sum p(x) \cdot v(x).$$

Then

$$g(p) = \sum p(x) \cdot (a + b \cdot u(x))$$
$$= a \cdot \sum p(x) + b \cdot \sum p(x) \cdot u(x) = a + b \cdot f(p),$$

since $\sum p(x) = 1$. Then, as u is a cardinal utility function for $\succeq$, $p \succeq q$ if and only if $f(p) \geq f(q)$ which obtains if and only if $g(p) \geq g(q)$ so that v is a cardinal utility function for $\succeq$. ∎

We write the degenerate lottery which assigns the probability of 1 to the outcome x as $[x]$ and the lottery r defined by

$$r = a \cdot p + (1 - a) \cdot q$$

where a is in $\mathbb{I}$ as $< p, q, a >$. We may interpret $< p, q, a >$ as a compound lottery: that is, as a lottery which gives as its outcomes the lottery p with the probability a and the lottery q with the probability $1 - a$.

Example 2.2. Let $X = \{x, y\}$ and let $a = 1/2$, $p(x) = 1$,

$$q(x) = q(y) = 1/2$$

and

$$r = a \cdot p + (1 - a) \cdot q.$$

Then $r(x) = 3/4$ and $r(y) = 1/4$. This example is illustrated in Figure 2.1. ∎

As the following example shows, not all orderings on the set P have the expected utility property.

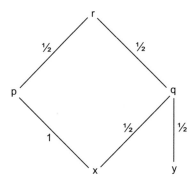

Figure 2.1

Example 2.3. Let

$$p = [x], \ q = [y], \ r = [z],$$

$$s = <p, r, a>, \ t = <q, r, a>$$

where $a \in \mathbb{I} \setminus \{0\}$ and let $\succeq$ be such that $p \succ q$ and $t \succ s$. If u is a cardinal utility function for $\succeq$ then $u(x) > u(y)$ and

$$a \cdot u(y) + (1 - a) \cdot u(z) > a \cdot u(x) + (1 - a) \cdot u(z)$$

so that $u(y) > u(x)$. It follows from this contradiction that $\succeq$ does not have the expected utility property. ∎

THE SUBSTITUTION AXIOM

The problem in Example 2.3 is that the lottery p is preferred to the lottery q but that q combined with some third lottery r is preferred to p combined with r in the same proportions. To avoid such problems we require that if one lottery is preferred to a second then any combination of the first lottery and some third lottery is preferred to the corresponding combination of the second lottery and the third. This requirement is the substitution axiom (also known as the independence axiom).

Definition. The ordering $\succeq$ on P satisfies the substitution axiom if, for all $p, q, r \in P$ and $a \in \mathbb{I} \setminus \{0\}$,

$$<p, r, a> \succeq <q, r, a>$$

if and only if $p \succeq q$. ∎

The remark below follows directly from this definition.

Remark. If the ordering $\succeq$ on P satisfies the substitution axiom then, for all $p, q, r \in P$ and $a \in \mathbb{I} \setminus \{0\}$:

$$<p, r, a> \succ <q, r, a>$$

38   *Rational Choice*

if and only if $p \succ q$; and

$$< p,r,a > \ \sim \ < q,r,a >$$

if and only if $p \sim q$. ∎

The following proposition shows that if an ordering satisfies the substitution axiom then it is increasing in probability: if one lottery is preferred to another then a combination of the two is preferred to a second combination if and only if the proportion of the better lottery in the first combination is greater than that in the second.

Proposition. If an ordering $\succeq$ on P satisfies the substitution axiom then it is increasing in probability: that is, for all p, $q \in P$ with $p \succ q$ and all $a, b \in$ 𝕀,

$$< p,q,a > \ \succ \ < p,q,b >$$

if and only if $a > b$. ∎

Proof. Let $p, q \in P$ with $p \succ q$. First, assume that $a > b$ and let

$$r = < p,q,a >.$$

Using the substitution axiom,

$$r \succ < q,q,a > = \ q.$$

Let

$$c = 1 - b/a > 0.$$

Then, by the substitution axiom,

$$r = \ < r,r,c > \ \succ \ < q,r,c >$$

and, from the construction of compound lotteries,

$$< q, r, c > = < p, q, b >.$$

Thus

$$< p, q, a > \succ < p, q, b >.$$

To prove the converse, assume that

$$< p, q, a > \succ < p, q, b >.$$

Then $b > a$ contradicts the result just established and $b = a$ contradicts the asymmetry of $\succ$; it follows that $a > b$. ∎

The substitution axiom also guarantees that there is a most preferred and a least preferred lottery, each of which is degenerate, as the following proposition shows.

Proposition. If an ordering $\succeq$ on P satisfies the substitution axiom then it is bounded: that is, there are $v, w \in X$ such that, for all $p \in P$,

$$[v] \succeq p \succeq [w]. ∎$$

Proof. As X is finite and $\succeq$ is an ordering there is some $v \in X$ such that $[v] \succeq [x]$ for all $x \in X$. Trivially, $[v] \succeq p$ for all $p \in P$ with support $\{v\}$. Now let $v \in G \subset X$, assume that $[v] \succeq p$ for all $p \in P$ with support G and let $H = G \cup \{y\}$ where $y \notin G$. If the support of p is H then there is some $q \in P$ with support G such that

$$p = < [y], q, a >,$$

this being defined by

$$q(x) = p(x)/(1 - a)$$

for all $x \in G$ where $a = p(y) > 0$. Then as $[v] \succeq [y]$ and $[v] \succeq q$, since the support of q is G, it follows, using the substitution axiom twice, that

$$[v] = <[v],[v],a> \succeq <[y],q,a> = p.$$

Thus $[v] \succeq p$ for all p with support H. It follows by induction that $[v] \succeq p$ for all $p \in P$. The existence of some $w \in X$ such that $p \succeq [w]$ for all $p \in P$ is demonstrated analogously. ∎

Even if an ordering satisfies the substitution axiom it may not have the expected utility property, as the following example shows.

Example 2.4. Let

$$p = [x], q = [y], r = [z], s = <p,r,a>$$

for arbitrary $a \in \mathbb{I}$ and let $\succeq$ be such that $p \succ q \succ r$ and $q \succ s$. Note that the substitution axiom is satisfied, trivially. Assume that u is a cardinal utility function for $\succeq$ such that, without loss of generality, $u(x) = 1$ and $u(z) = 0$. Then $1 > u(y) > 0$ so that $u(y) \in \mathbb{I}$; also,

$$u(y) > a \cdot 1 + (1 - a) \cdot 0 = a$$

for all $a \in \mathbb{I}$. It follows from this contradiction that $\succeq$ does not have the expected utility property. ∎

THE CONTINUITY AXIOM

The problem in Example 2.4 is that the lottery q lies between the lotteries p and r in preference but is preferred to all combinations of p and r: that is, there is no probability, however high, such that the compound lottery giving the better lottery with this high probability and the worse lottery with the corresponding low probability is at least as good as the intermediate lottery. To avoid such problems we require that if one lottery is preferred to a second and the second is preferred to a third then there is some combination of the first and the third which is indifferent to the second. This requirement is the continuity axiom (also known as the archimedean axiom).

Definition. The ordering $\succeq$ on P satisfies the continuity axiom if, for all $p, q, r \in P$ such that $p \succ q \succ r$,

$$q \sim <p, r, a>$$

for some $a \in \mathbb{I}$. ∎

The substitution and continuity axioms are independent. The ordering in Example 2.3 satisfies the continuity axiom, trivially, but fails to satisfy the substitution axiom; and the ordering in Example 2.4 satisfies the substitution axiom, as was noted, but fails to satisfy the continuity axiom. Examples of orderings which satisfy both axioms and of those which satisfy neither are obvious.

The remark below, which notes that the indifferent lottery in the definition of the continuity axiom is unique, follows from the fact that preference is increasing in probability.

Remark. If the ordering $\succeq$ on P satisfies the continuity axiom then, for all $p, q, r \in P$ with $p \succ q \succ r$,

$$q \sim <p, r, a>$$

for some unique $a \in \mathbb{I}$. ∎

The substitution and continuity axioms together ensure that the set of cardinal utility functions is restricted. Specifically, any cardinal utility function is an affine transformation of another; equivalently, each cardinal utility function is unique up to an affine transformation.

Proposition. If u and v are cardinal utility functions for an ordering $\succeq$ on P which satisfies the substitution and continuity axioms then there is some $a \in \mathbb{Q}$ and $b \in \mathbb{Q}\backslash\{0\}$ such that $v = a + b \cdot u$. ∎

Proof. Using boundedness, choose $s, t \in P$ such that $s \succeq p \succeq t$ for all $p \in P$. If $s \sim t$ then define u and v by $u(x) = 0$ and $v(x) = a$ and the requirement is satisfied trivially. Assume, then, that $s \succ t$ and define the functions f and g from P to $\mathbb{Q}$ by

$$f(p) = \sum p(x) \cdot u(x)$$

and

$$g(p) = \sum p(x) \cdot v(x);$$

note that if $a \in \mathbb{I}$ then

$$f(a \cdot p + (1 - a) \cdot q) = a \cdot f(p) + (1 - a) \cdot f(q)$$

and similarly for g. Without loss of generality, let $f(s) = 1$ and $f(t) = 0$; also, let $a = g(t)$ and

$$b = g(s) - g(t) > 0.$$

If $p \in P$ then, by the continuity axiom,

$$p \sim < s, t, c >$$

for some $c \in \mathbb{I}$ so that

$$f(p) = c \cdot f(s) + (1 - c) \cdot f(t) = c$$

and thus

$$g(p) = c \cdot g(s) + (1 - c) \cdot g(t)$$
$$= a + b \cdot c = a + b \cdot f(p).$$

Now if $x \in X$ and $p = [x]$ then

$$v(x) = g([x]) = a + b \cdot f([x]) = a + b \cdot u(x).$$

Thus $v = a + b \cdot u$. ∎

As the set P is infinite an arbitrary ordering on P may not have a utility representation. However, as the following proposition shows, the substitution and continuity axioms together ensure that such an ordering does have a utility representation and, further, that it has a linear utility representation. (A function f from the set of lotteries to $\mathbb{Q}$ is linear if the value which it assigns to a combination of two lotteries is equal to the same combination of the values which it assigns to each lottery individually.) A utility representation for $\succeq$ is not to be confused with the cardinal utility function invoked by $\succeq$: the former is defined on P and the latter on X.

Proposition. If an ordering $\succeq$ on P satisfies the substitution and continuity axioms then it has a linear utility representation: that is, there is a function f from P to $\mathbb{Q}$ such that, for all $p, q \in P$, $f(p) \geq f(q)$ if and only if $p \succeq q$ and, for all $a \in \mathbb{I}$,

$$f(a \cdot p + (1 - a) \cdot q) = a \cdot f(p) + (1 - a) \cdot f(q). \quad \blacksquare$$

Proof. Using boundedness, choose $s, t \in P$ such that $s \succeq p \succeq t$ for all $p \in P$ and, using the continuity axiom, define the function f from P to $\mathbb{Q}$ by

$$p \sim\, < s, t, f(p) >.$$

Then $f(p) \geq f(q)$ if and only if

$$< s, t, f(p) > \,\succeq\, < s, t, f(q) >,$$

as preference is increasing in probability; this obtains if and only if $p \succeq q$ so that f is a utility representation for $\succeq$. For all $p, q \in P$ and $a \in \mathbb{I}$,

$$< p, q, a > \,\sim\, \ll s, t, f(p) >, < s, t, f(q) >, a > \,=\, < s, t, c >$$

where

$$c = a \cdot f(p) + (1 - a) \cdot f(q).$$

Then

$$f(<p, q, a >) = f(a \cdot p + (1 - a) \cdot q)$$

and also

$$f(<p, q, a >) = f(< s, t, c >)$$
$$= c = a \cdot f(p) + (1 - a) \cdot f(q).$$

It follows that

$$f(a \cdot p + (1 - a) \cdot q) = a \cdot f(p) + (1 - a) \cdot f(q)$$

so that f is linear. ∎

THE EXPECTED UTILITY PROPERTY

The following two propositions show that an ordering has the expected utility property if and only if it satisfies the substitution and continuity axioms.

Proposition. If an ordering $\succeq$ on P has the expected utility property then it satisfies the substitution and continuity axioms. ∎

Proof. Define the function f from P to $\mathbb{Q}$ by

$$f(p) = \sum p(x) \cdot u(x)$$

where u is a cardinal utility function for $\succeq$ and let $p, q, r \in P$ and $a \in \mathbb{I} \setminus \{0\}$; note that f is a linear utility representation for $\succeq$. Then $p \succeq q$ if and only if $f(p) \geq f(q)$ which obtains if and only if

$$a \cdot f(p) + (1 - a) \cdot f(r) \geq a \cdot f(q) + (1 - a) \cdot f(r)$$

which obtains if and only if

$$f(<p,r,a>) \geq f(<q,r,a>)$$

which obtains if and only if

$$<p,r,a> \succeq <q,r,a>$$

so that the substitution axiom is satisfied. Now if $p \succ q \succ r$ and

$$a = (f(q) - f(r))/(f(p) - f(r))$$

then

$$f(q) = a \cdot f(p) + (1-a) \cdot f(r) = f(<p,r,a>)$$

so that $q \sim <p,r,a>$ and the continuity axiom is satisfied. ∎

Proposition. If an ordering $\succeq$ on P satisfies the substitution and continuity axioms then it has the expected utility property. ∎

Proof. Let f be a linear utility representation for $\succeq$ and define the function u from X to $\mathbb{Q}$ by $u(x) = f([x])$. Let $z \in X$; then, trivially,

$$f(p) = \sum p(x) \cdot u(x)$$

for all $p \in P$ with support $\{z\}$. Now let $G \subset X$, assume that

$$f(p) = \sum p(x) \cdot u(x)$$

for all $p \in P$ with support G and let $H = G \cup \{y\}$ where $y \notin G$. If the support of p is H then there is some $q \in P$ with support G such that

$$p = <[y], q, a>$$

this being defined by

$$q(x) = p(x)/(1 - a)$$

for all $x \in G$ where $a = p(y) > 0$. Then, as f is linear,

$$
\begin{aligned}
f(p) &= a \cdot f([y]) + (1 - a) \cdot f(q) \\
&= p(y) \cdot f([y]) + (1 - p(y)) \cdot f(q) \\
&= p(y) \cdot u(y) + (1 - a) \cdot \sum [x \in G] \, q(x) \cdot u(x) \\
&= p(y) \cdot u(y) + (1 - a) \cdot \sum [x \in G](p(x)/(1 - a)) \cdot u(x) \\
&= p(y) \cdot u(y) + \sum [x \in G] \, p(x) \cdot u(x) \\
&= \sum [x \in H] \, p(x) \cdot u(x) = \sum p(x) \cdot u(x).
\end{aligned}
$$

Since this applies for all $p \in P$ with support H it follows by induction that

$$f(p) = \sum p(x) \cdot u(x)$$

for all $p \in P$ so that $p \succeq q$ if and only if

$$\sum p(x) \cdot u(x) \geq \sum q(x) \cdot u(x).$$

Thus $\succeq$ has the expected utility property. ∎

The preceding two propositions give the following characterisation of the set of rational choice rules.

Remark. A choice rule on the family of uncertainty problems is rational if and only if it has a reason which satisfies the substitution and continuity axioms. ∎

SUBJECTIVE PROBABILITY

The preceding discussion concerns choice under uncertainty with given probabilities. We now turn to choice under uncer-

tainty where probabilities are not given. As some of the
proofs are lengthy, and to some extent analogous to the
proofs for the case with given probabilities, we discuss this
case only informally.

There is now a second source of uncertainty, the state of the
world. A state, like an event, is a description of some aspect of
the physical universe: for example, one state may be that it is
raining and another that the sun is shining. States are defined in
such a way that precisely one must occur. They are independent
of events: it may or may not rain when a coin displays heads,
and a coin may or may not display heads when it is raining.

If probabilities are given then a lottery is completely determined by my act. In the present framework, however, a
lottery is determined both by my act and the state that occurs:
that is, I am given, as well as a set of acts, a finite set of states
and a rule f which specifies the lottery $f(a,s)$ which obtains if I
choose the act a and the state s occurs. This means that
choosing an act is equivalent to choosing a rule which specifies the lottery which is obtained in each state. More precisely, choosing an act a is equivalent to choosing the
function $h(\cdot;a)$ from the set S of states to the set P of lotteries
defined by

$$h(s;a) = f(a,s).$$

We may then interpret the present problem as being that of
choosing over the set H of functions from S to P; we refer to
such functions as prospects.

Given some prospect h and some state s the value $h(s)$ is a
probability distribution: it specifies the probability of each
outcome conditional on the state s occurring. Thus $h(s)(x)$ is
the probability of obtaining the outcome x given the state s.

My choice over the set of prospects is rational if I can
assign a subjective probability $m(s)$ to each state s and a
cardinal utility to each outcome in such a way that choosing
over prospects is equivalent to maximising expected utility
calculated using these subjective probabilities. Note that the
probability of obtaining the outcome x if I choose the

prospect h is the sum over all states s of the objective probability of obtaining x if s occurs multiplied by the subjective probability of s occurring: that is,

$$\sum [s \in S]\ (h(s)(x)) \cdot m(s).$$

Thus choice is rational if there is a probability distribution m on S and a cardinal utility function u defined on X such that chosen prospects maximise

$$\sum [x \in X] \sum [s \in S]\ (h(x)(s)) \cdot m(s) \cdot u(x)$$

over h in H.

As with lotteries, combinations of prospects are also prospects: that is, if f and g are prospects then so is the combination h defined by

$$h = a \cdot f + (1 - a) \cdot g$$

where a is in $\mathbb{I}$; this prospect is written as $\ll f, g, a \gg$.

A necessary condition for choice to be rational is that it has a transitive reason. We propose two axioms concerning such a reason.

The first axiom is analogous to the substitution axiom. It requires that if one prospect is preferred to a second then any combination of the first prospect and some third prospect is preferred to the corresponding combination of the second and the third. More precisely,

$$\ll f, h, a \gg\ \succeq\ \ll g, h, a \gg$$

if and only if $f \succeq g$ for all prospects h and all a in $\mathbb{I}\backslash 0\}$.

The second axiom is analogous to the continuity axiom. It requires that if one prospect is preferred to a second and the second to a third then there is some combination of the first and the third which is indifferent to the second. More precisely, if $f \succ g \succ h$ then there is some a in $\mathbb{I}$ such that

$g \sim \ll f, h, a \gg.$

These two axioms together are necessary and sufficient for there to be cardinal utility functions for each state such that one prospect is preferred to a second if and only if it has a higher expected utility. More precisely, there is, for each state s, a function $v(.;s)$ from the set of outcomes to $\mathbb{Q}$ such that, for any two prospects f and g, $f \succeq g$ if and only if

$$\sum [x \in X] \sum [s \in S] \, (f(s)(x)) \cdot v(x;s)$$

$$\geq \sum [x \in X] \sum [s \in S] \, (g(s)(x)) \cdot v(x;s).$$

Further, each function $v(.;s)$, which is a state-dependent cardinal utility function, is unique up to an affine transformation.

STATE-INDEPENDENT UTILITY

The representation which we have obtained, though useful, is weaker than the representation which we seek. The difference between the two is that in the former, which is a state-dependent representation, subjective probabilities and underlying utilities are implicitly combined in an arbitrary way in the state-dependent cardinal utility functions $v(.;s)$. In the latter, which is a state-independent representation, they are explicitly combined in a multiplicative way: that is, there is a probability distribution m on the set of states and a cardinal utility function u defined on the set of outcomes such that

$$v(x;s) = m(s) \cdot u(x)$$

for each outcome x and state s.

The existence of a state-dependent representation does not imply that of a state-independent representation, as the following example shows.

Example 2.5. Let x, $y \in X$ and s, $t \in S$ and let the state-dependent cardinal utility functions $v(.;s)$ and $v(.;t)$ be specified by

$$v(x;s) = 0, \ v(x;t) = 1,$$
$$v(y;s) = 1, \ v(y;t) = 0.$$

If there is some probability a and some state-independent cardinal utility function u such that

$$v(x;s) = a \cdot u(x), \ v(x;t) = (1-a) \cdot u(x),$$
$$v(y;s) = a \cdot u(y), \ v(y;t) = (1-a) \cdot u(y)$$

then $a \cdot u(x) = 0$ and

$$(1-a) \cdot u(x) = 1$$

so that $a = 0$; and

$$(1-a) \cdot u(y) = 0$$

and $a \cdot u(y) = 1$ so that $a = 1$. It follows from this contradiction that there are no such a and u. ■

To obtain a state-independent representation we introduce a further axiom. This involves the concept of a null state: that is, one which can effectively be ignored. A state s is null if $f \sim g$ for all prospects f and g such that $f(t) = g(t)$ for all states t other than s. If a state is null then its state-dependent cardinal utility function, if it has one, is constant. Our further axiom requires that not all prospects are indifferent, and that if some lottery is better than a second in some state then it is better in all non-null states.

This third axiom may be stated more precisely as follows. For any prospect h, lottery p and state t let $d(h, p, t)$ be the prospect which takes the value p for the state t and the value

$h(s)$ for all states s other than t. Then the axiom requires that there are prospects f and g such that $f \succ g$ and, for all prospects h and all lotteries p and q, if

$$d(h, p, t) \succ d(h, q, t)$$

for some state t then

$$d(h, p, s) \succ d(h, q, s)$$

for all non-null states s.

The first part of this axiom excludes trivialities. The substantive part implies that orderings are independent of states. Thus if an umbrella is preferred to a sola topi when it is raining then an umbrella is preferred to a sola topi when the sun is shining. This is a strong requirement.

The three axioms presented above are necessary and sufficient for there to be subjective probabilities and state-independent underlying utilities such that one prospect is preferred to a second if and only if it has a higher expected utility. More precisely, there is a probability distribution m on S and a function u from X to $\mathbb{Q}$ such that, for all prospects f and g, $f \succeq g$ if and only if

$$\sum [x \in X] \sum [s \in S] \, (f(s)(x)) \cdot m(s) \cdot u(s)$$

$$\geq \sum [x \in X] \sum [s \in S] \, (g(s)(x)) \cdot m(s) \cdot u(s).$$

Further, the function u is unique up to an affine transformation.

The theory developed above is in the context of states and events. It may immediately be applied in the context of states alone by restricting attention to degenerate lotteries. Alternatively, the theory in this context can be developed directly, without recourse to events. However, this direct approach requires that the set of outcomes be infinite (and uncountable).

Notes

The axiomatic analysis of choice under uncertainty is due to von Neumann and Morgenstern (1944); a simpler analysis is provided by Luce and Raiffa (1957).

The discussion of uncertainty which involves both events and states follows that of Anscombe and Aumann (1963), who provide proofs of the assertions made in this context; a single-stage simplification of this approach is given by Sarin and Wakker (1997). The direct treatment which involves only states is developed by Savage (1954), drawing on the work of Ramsey (1931).

Surveys covering some of the material discussed in this chapter and various extensions to this are provided by Fishburn (1970) and Kreps (1988).

3 Risk

We digress from our main theme to discuss the attitudes to risk which are embodied in choice under uncertainty. We first define risk aversion and propose a measure of this. We then consider how the attitudes to risk embodied in different choice rules may be compared.

NUMBER LOTTERIES

Choices over lotteries involve attitudes to risk as well as preferences over outcomes. The former are displayed most clearly when outcomes can be identified with numbers, such as amounts of money. Accordingly, we consider the case where the set of outcomes, which we now write as X^*, comprises all the rational numbers up to some limit, which, without loss of generality, we take to be 4. (We set this limit as 4 rather than the more natural level of 1 simply to avoid having to deal with fractions.) This is a departure from the framework of Chapter 2 since the set of outcomes is no longer finite. However, this set is countable as it is a subset of $\mathbb{Q}$. We write the set of probability distributions on the set X^*, or number lotteries, as P^*.

Definition. The set P^* of number lotteries is the set of probability distributions on

$$X^* = \{x \in \mathbb{Q} : 4 \geq x\}. \quad \blacksquare$$

As the set of outcomes is not finite we cannot use the results established in Chapter 2. It remains the case that if choices on the set of lotteries are rational then there is an ordering $\succeq$ on this set such that chosen lotteries are maximal with respect to $\succeq$. This is because choice on the set of all lotteries can only be rational if choice on any finite subset is rational, which in

Rational Choice

turn requires that there is such an ordering. However, we cannot assume that this ordering $\succeq$ has the expected utility property: that is, that there is a cardinal utility function for $\succeq$. Accordingly, the discussion does not depend on the existence of a cardinal utility function, though does from time to time indicate what would obtain if there were such a function.

We assume that orderings satisfy the substitution and continuity axioms as defined in Chapter 2. We also assume that preference is covering, in that there is some degenerate lottery which is indifferent to any nondegenerate lottery; and that preference is monotone, in that larger outcomes are preferred to smaller. An ordering with these properties is a *regular ordering*.

Definition. The ordering $\succeq$ on P^* is regular if:

(a) for all $p, q, r \in P^*$ and $a \in \mathbb{I} \setminus \{0\}$,

$$< p, r, a > \; \succeq \; < q, r, a >$$

if and only if $p \succeq q$ (the substitution axiom);

(b) for all $p, q, r \in P^*$ such that $p \succ q \succ r$,

$$q \sim < p, r, a >$$

for some $a \in \mathbb{I}$ (the continuity axiom);

(c) for all $p \in P^*$, there is some $x \in X^*$ such that $[x] \sim p$ (the covering property); and

(d) for all $x, y \in X^*$, $[x] \succeq [y]$ if and only if $x \geq y$ (the monotone property). ∎

The following example shows that neither the monotone property nor the covering property is implied by the substitution and continuity axioms.

Example 3.1. Let the ordering $\succeq$ on P^* be specified by $p \succeq q$ if and only if

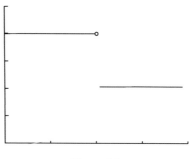

Figure 3.1

$$\sum p(x) \cdot f(x) \geq \sum q(x) \cdot f(x)$$

where $f(x) = 2$ if $2 \geq x$ and $f(x) = 1$ if $x > 2$. Then f is a cardinal utility function for $\succeq$ so that $\succeq$ satisfies the substitution and continuity axioms. However, $[0] \succ [4]$ so that $\succeq$ is not monotone; and there is no $x \in X^*$ such that

$$[x] \sim < [0], [4], 1/2 >$$

so that $\succeq$ is not covering. This example is illustrated in Figure 3.1. ■

RISK AVERSION

Consider two lotteries: the nondegenerate lottery giving the two outcomes 0 and 2 with equal probability and thus whose mathematical expectation is 1; and the degenerate lottery giving the outcome 1. Assume that I prefer larger outcomes to smaller. Then if I am risk averse I will prefer the degenerate lottery, if I am risk neutral I will be indifferent between the two, and if I am risk seeking I will prefer the nondegenerate lottery. We discuss only the first of these three cases, that of risk aversion; the remaining two cases may be treated analogously.

The expectation of the lottery p, which we denote by $e(p)$, is $\sum p(x) \cdot x$. We define an ordering to be risk averse if, for any nondegenerate lottery p, the degenerate lottery whose outcome is $e(p)$ is preferred to p.

Definition. The regular ordering $\succeq$ on P^* is risk averse if $[e(p)] \succ p$, where

$$e(p) = \sum p(x) \cdot x,$$

for all nondegenerate $p \in P^*$. ∎

Equivalently, an ordering is risk averse if its cardinal utility function u, if it has one, is such that the utility of the expectation of a lottery p is greater than the expected utility of p: that is, if

$$u(e(p)) > \sum u(x) \cdot p(x).$$

Example 3.2. Let $\succeq$ have the cardinal utility function u such that

$$u(0) = 0, \ u(1) = 2, \ u(2) = 3.$$

If

$$p = < [2], [0], 1/2 >$$

then $e(p) = 1$ and

$$u(1) > (1/2) \cdot u(2) + (1/2) \cdot u(0)$$

so that, at least on $\{0, 1, 2\}$, $\succeq$ is risk averse. This example is illustrated in Figure 3.2. ∎

A binary lottery is a nondegenerate lottery of the form $< [x], [z], a >$; and an ordering is binary risk averse if, for any binary lottery p, the degenerate lottery whose outcome

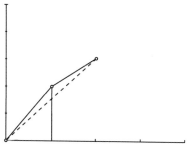

Figure 3.2

is *e(p)* is preferred to *p*. It is clear that risk aversion implies binary risk aversion; the following proposition shows that these two properties are equivalent.

Proposition. The regular ordering $\succeq$ on P^* is risk averse if and only if it is binary risk averse: that is, if and only if

$$[a \cdot x + (1 - a) \cdot z] \succ \; < [x], [z], a >$$

for all $x, z \in X^*$ and $a \in \mathbb{I}$ with $1 > a > 0$. ∎

Proof. First, note that as a property which is satisfied for every lottery is satisfied for every binary lottery risk aversion implies binary risk aversion. To prove the converse, assume that $\succeq$ is binary risk averse and let $x, y, z \in X^*$ with

$$x > y = a \cdot x + (1 - a) \cdot z > z$$

and

$$p = \; < [x], [z], a >;$$

note that $1 > a > 0$. Then, as $\succeq$ is binary risk averse,

$$[e(p)] = [y] \succ \; < [x], [z], a > \; = \; p.$$

This is to say that $[e(p)] \succ p$ for all $p \in P^*$ with support $\{x, z\}$. Now let $G \subset X^*$, assume that $[e(p)] \succ p$ for all $p \in P^*$ with support G and let $H = G \cup \{w\}$ where $w \notin G$. If the support of p is H then there is some $q \in P^*$ with support G such that

$$p = \; < [w], q, c >,$$

this being defined by

$$q(v) = p(v)/(1 - c)$$

for all $v \in G$ where $c = p(w) > 0$. Then

$$[e(p)] = [c \cdot w + (1 - c).e(q)] \; \succ \; < [w], [e(q)], c >$$

because $\succeq$ is binary risk averse; and

$$< [w], [e(q)], c > \; \succ \; < [w], q, c > \; = p$$

because $[e(q)] \succ q$. Thus $[e(p)] \succ p$ for all $p \in P^*$ with support H. Since the support of each $p \in P^*$ is finite it follows by induction that $[e(p)] \succ p$ for all nondegenerate $p \in P^*$ which is to say that $\succeq$ is risk averse. ∎

THE PROBABILITY RISK PREMIUM

Consider the outcomes x, y and z where

$$x > y = a \cdot x + (1 - a) \cdot z > z$$

for some a in $\mathbb{I}$ and note that the expectation of the lottery

$$p = \; < [x], [z], a >$$

is y. We may consider a to be the fair probability (for the better outcome) in a lottery on x and z relative to y. Now because of the continuity axiom there is some unique b in $\mathbb{I}$ such that the lottery $< [x], [z], b >$ is indifferent to the degenerate lottery $[y]$. We may consider b to be the indifference-equivalent probability (for the better outcome) in a lottery on x and z relative to y. The excess of the indifference-equivalent probability over the fair probability (that is, $b - a$) is the probability risk premium.

Definition. The probability risk premium $r(x, y, z)$ for the regular ordering $\succeq$ on P^* where $x, y, z \in X^*$ with $x > y > z$ is defined by

$$< [x], [z], a + r(x, y, z) > \sim [y]$$

where $a \in \mathbb{I}$ is such that

$$y = a \cdot x + (1 - a) \cdot z;$$

$\succeq$ has a positive probability risk premium if

$$r(x, y, z) > 0$$

for all $x, y, z \in X^*$. ∎

Note that, in the notation employed in this definition,

$$a + r(x, y, z) \in \mathbb{I}$$

and also that, for all $b \in \mathbb{I}$,

$$< [x], [z], b > \succ [y]$$

if and only if

$$b - a > r(x, y, z).$$

Equivalently, the probability risk premium $r(x, y, z)$ for an ordering with the cardinal utility function u is $b - a$ where a is such that

$$y = a \cdot x + (1 - a) \cdot z$$

and b is such that

$$u(y) = b \cdot u(x) + (1 - b) \cdot u(z).$$

Example 3.3. Let $\succeq$ have the cardinal utility function u such that

$$u(0) = 0, \ u(1) = 2, \ u(3) = 3.$$

Then

$$1 = (1/3) \cdot 3 + (2/3) \cdot 0$$

and

$$u(1) = (2/3) \cdot u(3) + (1/3) \cdot u(0)$$

so that

$$r(3, 1, 0) = 2/3 - 1/3 = 1/3.$$

This example is illustrated in Figure 3.3. ∎

The two remarks below follow from the definition of the probability risk premium and from the equivalence between risk aversion and binary risk aversion, respectively.

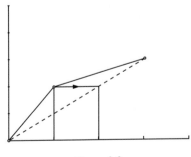

Figure 3.3

Remark. A regular ordering on P^* has a positive probability risk premium if and only if it is binary risk averse. ∎

Remark. A regular ordering on P^* has a positive probability risk premium if and only if it is risk averse. ∎

THE OUTCOME RISK PREMIUM

Consider again the outcomes x, y and z where

$$x > y = a \cdot x + (1 - a) \cdot z > z$$

for some a in $\mathbb{I}$; as before, the expectation of the lottery

$$p = < [x], [z], a >$$

is y. Because of the covering property there is some unique outcome w such that p is indifferent to the degenerate lottery $[w]$. We may consider w to be the indifference-equivalent outcome corresponding to p. The excess of the expectation over the indifference-equivalent outcome (that is, $y - w$) is the outcome risk premium.

Definition. The outcome risk premium $s(x, y, z)$ for the regular ordering $\succeq$ on P^* where $x, y, z \in X^*$ with $x > y > z$ is defined by

$$[y - s(x, y, z)] \sim < [x], [z], a >$$

where $a \in \mathbb{I}$ is such that

$$y = a \cdot x + (1 - a) \cdot z;$$

$\succeq$ has a positive outcome risk premium if

$$s(x, y, z) > 0$$

for all $x, y, z \in X^*$.

Note that, in the notation employed in this definition,

$$y - s(x, y, z) \in X^*$$

and, further, that

$$x > y - s(x, y, z) > z.$$

Equivalently, the outcome risk premium $s(x, y, z)$ for an ordering with the cardinal utility function u is given by

$$u(y - s(x, y, z)) = a \cdot u(x) + (1 - a) \cdot u(z)$$

where a is such that

$$y = a \cdot x + (1 - a) \cdot z.$$

Example 3.4. Let $\succeq$ have the cardinal utility function u specified in Example 3.3. Then

$$2 = (2/3) \cdot 3 + (1/3) \cdot 0$$

and

$$u(2 - 1) = (2/3) \cdot u(3) + (1/3) \cdot u(0)$$

so that

$$s(3, 2, 0) = 1.$$

This example is illustrated in Figure 3.4. ■

The following proposition shows that there is a simple relationship between the two risk premiums, r and s: the outcome premium s at (x, y, z) is the probability premium r at

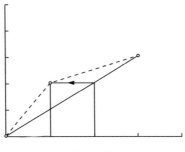

Figure 3.4

$$(x, y - s, z)$$

expressed in terms of outcomes.

Proposition. If $x, y, z \in X^*$ and $r(x, y, z)$ and $s(x, y, z)$ are the probability and outcome risk premiums, respectively, for the regular ordering $\succeq$ on P^* then

$$s(x, y, z) = (x - z) \cdot r(x, y - s(x, y, z), z).\ \blacksquare$$

Proof. Write $s(x, y, z)$ as s and $r(x, y - s, z)$ as r. Then

$$s = (x - z) \cdot r$$

if and only if

$$< [x], [z], a > \ \sim\ [y - s] = [y - (x - z) \cdot r]$$
$$= [(a - r) \cdot x + (1 - (a - r)) \cdot z]$$

since

$$y = a \cdot x + (1 - a) \cdot z.$$

Writing $a - r$ as b this condition is

$$< [x], [z], b + r > \ \sim\ [b \cdot x + (1 - b) \cdot z] = [y - s],$$

which holds because

$$r = r(x, y - s, z). \blacksquare$$

Example 3.5. Let $\succeq$ have the cardinal utility function u specified in Example 3.3. Then

$$s(3,2,0) = (3 - 0) \cdot r(3, 2 - 1, 0)$$

using the values for $r(3, 1, 0)$ and $s(3, 2, 0)$ obtained in Examples 3.3 and 3.4. $\blacksquare$

It follows from the preceding proposition that the probability risk premium is everywhere positive if and only if the outcome risk premium is everywhere positive. The remark below follows from this observation and the preceding remark.

Remark. A regular ordering on P^* has a positive outcome risk premium if and only if it is risk averse. $\blacksquare$

COMPARATIVE RISK AVERSION

We now consider two orderings, one for me and one for you. We say that I am more risk averse than you if you would accept any risk which I would accept but not conversely. More precisely, I am more risk averse than you if whenever I am indifferent between some nondegenerate lottery p and some degenerate lottery $[x]$ you prefer p to $[x]$.

Definition. The regular ordering $\succeq$ on P^* is more risk averse than the regular ordering $\succeq'$ on P^* if, for all $x \in X^*$ and nondegenerate $p \in P^*$, $p \sim [x]$ implies that $p \succ' [x]$. $\blacksquare$

Equivalently, the ordering $\succeq$ with the cardinal utility function u is more risk averse than the ordering $\succeq'$ with the cardinal utility function u' if

$$\sum p(x) \cdot u(x) = u(y)$$

implies that

$$\sum p(x) \cdot u'(x) > u'(y)$$

for all lotteries p and outcomes y.

Example 3.6. Let the regular orderings $\succeq$ and $\succeq'$ on P^* have the cardinal utility functions u and u' specified in the matrix

x	0	1	2
u	0	4	5
u'	0	3	5

Note that both $\succeq$ and $\succeq'$ are risk averse, at least on $\{0, 1, 2\}$. Then, as may be verified, $\succeq$ is more risk averse than $\succeq'$, at least on $\{0, 1, 2\}$. This example is illustrated in Figure 3.5. ∎

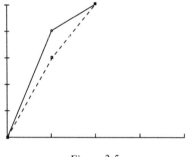

Figure 3.5

The following two propositions show that one ordering is more risk averse than a second if and only if the probability risk premium for the first everywhere exceeds that for the second. They thus provide a justification for interpreting the probability risk premium as a measure of risk aversion.

Proposition. If the regular ordering $\succeq$ on P^* with the probability risk premium r is more risk averse than the regular ordering $\succeq'$ on P^* with the probability risk premium r' then r exceeds r' everywhere: that is,

$$r(x, y, z) > r'(x, y, z)$$

for all $x, y, z \in X^*$. ∎

Proof. Let $x, y, z \in X^*$ with

$$x > y = a \cdot x + (1 - a) \cdot z > z$$

and

$$p = < [x], [z], b >$$

for some $b \in \mathbb{I}$. Assume that $p \sim [y]$ implies that $p \succ' [y]$. Now $p \sim [y]$ if and only if

$$b - a = r(x, y, z),$$

and $p \succ' [y]$ if and only if

$$b - a > r'(x, y, z).$$

It follows that

$$r(x, y, z) > r'(x, y, z)$$

so that r exceeds r' everywhere. ∎

Proposition. The regular ordering $\succeq$ on P^* with the probability risk premium r is more risk averse than the regular ordering $\succeq'$ on P^* with the probability risk premium r' if r exceeds r' everywhere. ∎

Proof. Assume that $r > r'$ everywhere and let $x, y, z \in X^*$ with

$$x > y = a \cdot x + (1 - a) \cdot z > z$$

and

$$p = < [x], [z], b >$$

for some $b \in \mathbb{I}$. Then $p \sim [y]$ if and only if

$$b - a = r(x, y, z),$$

and $p \succ' [y]$ if and only if

$$b - a > r'(x, y, z);$$

thus $p \sim [y]$ implies that $p \succ' [y]$. It follows that $p \sim [y]$ implies that $p \succ' [y]$ for all (nondegenerate) $p \in P^*$ with support $\{x, z\}$. Now let $G \subset X^*$, assume that $p \sim [y]$ implies that $p \succ' [y]$ for all nondegenerate $p \in P^*$ with support G and let $H = G \cup \{w\}$ where $w \notin G$. If the support of p is H then there is some $q \in P^*$ with support G such that

$$p = <[w], q, c>,$$

this being defined by

$$q(t) = p(t)/(1 - c)$$

for all $t \in G$ where $c = p(w) > 0$. Using the covering property, let $u \in X^*$ be such that $q \sim [u]$; then $q \succ' [u]$. Also let $v \in X^*$ be such that $p \sim [v]$ and $d \in \mathbb{I}$ be such that

$$v = d \cdot w + (1 - d) \cdot u.$$

If $w \geq u$ then

$$c - d = r(w, v, u) > r'(w, v, u)$$

because

$$p \sim <[w], [u], c> \sim [v];$$

this implies that

$$<[w], [u], c> \succ' [v].$$

Analogously, if $u > w$, then

$$(1 - c) - (1 - d) = r(u, v, w) > r'(u, v, w)$$

which implies that

$$< [u], [w], 1 - c > = < [w], [u], c > \succ' [v].$$

Then, as $q \succ' [u]$,

$$p = < [w], q, c > \succ' < [w], [u], c > \succ' [v].$$

Since this holds for all $p \in P^*$ with support H, and as the support of all $p \in P^*$ is finite, it follows by induction that $p \sim [v]$ implies that $p \succ' [v]$ for all nondegenerate $p \in P^*$ which is to say that $\succeq$ is more risk averse than $\succeq'$. ∎

The remark below follows from the preceding two propositions and the relationship between the two measures of risk premium. It provides a justification for interpreting the outcome risk premium, as well as the probability risk premium, as a measure of risk aversion.

Remark. The regular ordering $\succeq$ on P^* with the outcome risk premium s is more risk averse than the regular ordering $\succeq'$ on P^* with the outcome risk premium s' if and only if s exceeds s' everywhere. ∎

It should be noted that it may be the case that neither is one ordering more risk averse than a second (distinct) ordering nor is the second more risk averse than the first. This is shown in the following example.

Example 3.7. Let the regular orderings $\succeq$ and $\succeq'$ on P^* have the cardinal utility functions u and u' specified in the matrix

x	0	1	2	3	4
u	0	8	12	15	17
u'	0	7	12	16	17

Note that both $\succeq$ and $\succeq'$ are risk averse, at least for the outcomes specified. However,

$$r(2,\ 1,\ 0) = 1/6 > 1/12 = r'(2,\ 1,\ 0)$$

and

$$r'(4,\ 3,\ 2) = 3/10 > 1/10 = r(4,\ 3,\ 2)$$

so is that neither is $\succeq$ more risk averse than $\succeq'$ nor is $\succeq'$ more risk averse than $\succeq$. This example is illustrated in Figure 3.6. ■

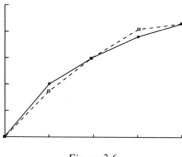

Figure 3.6

Notes

The measurement of risk aversion originates in the work of Pratt (1964) and Arrow (1971). However, the standard Arrow–Pratt framework requires the existence of a cardinal utility function and also assumes that this is, in a mathematical sense, smooth.

A survey of risk aversion in this smooth framework is provided by Kreps (1988).

4 Strategy

We address the problem of strategic choice, as a generalisation of the problem of choice under uncertainty. We first set out the problem, propose a definition of rationality and provide a characterisation of the choice rules which are rational. We conclude by discussing two alternative approaches to the strategy problem.

STRATEGY PROBLEMS

The problem addressed in Chapter 2 was that of choosing an act the result of which depends on some event that occurs by chance, or, more poetically, on some act that is chosen blindly by Nature. I am given a probability distribution on the set of Nature's acts: my choice is rational if I have a cardinal utility function defined on the set of outcomes, or, equivalently, on the product of my and Nature's sets of acts, such that the acts that I choose are those which yield the highest expected utility given this probability distribution.

We now turn to the more general problem of my choosing an act the result of which depends on some act chosen deliberately by Nature as well as on the act that I choose: that is, where both I and Nature choose rationally. I and Nature each know that we each choose rationally, we each know that we each know that we each choose rationally, and so forth.

As a consequence of the interrelation between my and Nature's problems we address the two symmetrically. I and Nature are each faced with a set of acts over which I choose, a corresponding set over which Nature chooses and a rule which associates some unique outcome with each pair of acts. As was established in Chapter 2, if I and Nature each choose rationally then we each have a cardinal utility function defined on the product of the two sets of acts.

71

A strategy problem is defined by these two sets and two cardinal utility functions. Note that an uncertainty problem is the special case of a strategy problem in which Nature is indifferent between all outcomes and chooses all acts with equal probability.

Definition. A strategy problem is specified by the array (A, A', u, u') where A and A' are nonempty finite sets and u and u' are cardinal utility functions on $A \times A'$. ■

Example 4.1. Let $A = \{a, b\}$, $A' = \{a', b'\}$ and u and u' be specified by the matrix

	a'	b'
a	2, 2	0, 3
b	3, 0	1, 1

(that is, let $u(a, b') = 0$ and $u'(a, b') = 3$, and so forth). Then (A, A', u, u') is a strategy problem. (This example is sometimes referred to as the prisoners' dilemma.) ■

A choice rule in the present context associates with each strategy problem a set of acts chosen by me and a set chosen by Nature.

Definition. A choice rule on the family of strategy problems is a function taking (A, A', u, u') to (C, C') where $C \subset A$ and $C' \subset A'$ are nonempty. ■

If I am given a probability distribution p' on the set of Nature's acts then I choose an act which maximises my expected utility given p'. Such an act is a best response, for my cardinal utility function, to the probability distribution p'.

Definition. In the strategy problem (A, A', u, u') $a \in A$ is a best response for u to the probability distribution p' on A' if

$$\sum p'(a') \cdot u(a, a') \geq \sum p'(a') \cdot u(b, a')$$

for all $b \in A$; a best response for u' is defined analogously. ∎

Example 4.2. Let $A = \{a, b\}$, $A' = \{a', b'\}$ and u and u' be specified by the matrix

	a'	b'
a	1, 1	0, 0
b	0, 0	1, 1

If $p'(a') > p'(b')$ then a is the sole best response (for u) to p'; if $p'(b') > p'(a')$ then b is the sole best response to p'; and if $p'(a') = p'(b')$ then a and b are both best responses to p'. (This example is sometimes referred to as meeting in New York.) ∎

We do not distinguish between a probability distribution on A whose support is contained in some subset S of A and a probability distribution on S: each distribution assigns a positive probability only to acts in S, though need not assign a positive probability to all acts in S. We write the set of such probability distributions as $P(S)$ and the set of probability distributions on a subset S' of A' as $P'(S')$. The response function V, for the cardinal utility function u, associates with each nonempty subset S' of A' the set of acts which are best responses, for this cardinal utility function, to some probability distribution on S'.

Definition. In the strategy problem (A, A', u, u') the response function for u takes each $S' \subset A'$ to the set of $a \in A$ which are best responses for u to some probability distribution on S'; the response function for u' is defined analogously. ∎

Example 4.3. Let (A, A', u, u') be specified as in Example 4.2 (meeting in New York) and V be the response function for u. Then

$$V(\{a'\}) = \{a\}, \quad V(\{b'\}) = \{b\}, \quad V(A') = A. \quad ∎$$

RATIONALITY AND RATIONALISABLE ACTS

In a strategy problem I do not know the probability distribution on Nature's set of acts. However, I may infer something about this probability distribution as I know that Nature chooses rationally. Specifically, I may infer that each act for Nature to which I assign a positive probability is a best response to some probability distribution on my set of acts. Further, as I know that Nature is rational, I should anticipate that Nature makes an analogous inference. Indeed, I should anticipate that Nature anticipates that I make an analogous inference, and so forth ad infinitum. The acts that I and Nature choose are rationalisable if they arise from our each following this chain of reasoning.

More precisely, if my choice is rationalisable then the act a that I choose is a best response to my belief: that is, to some probability distribution on A'. This is to say that a is in $V(A')$, which set we write as $L(1)$. Also, I expect Nature's act to be in the set $L'(1)$, defined analogously. This means that my belief should only assign positive probability to those of Nature's acts which are in $L'(1)$ so that a is a best response to some probability distribution on $L'(1)$. This is to say that a is in $V(L'(1))$, which set we write as $L(2)$. Further, I expect Nature's act to be in the set $L'(2)$, defined analogously. This chain of reasoning leads to the following definition of the sets of rationalisable acts.

Definition. In the strategy problem (A, A', u, u') the rationalisable sets are

$$L = L(1) \cap L(2) \cap \cdots \subset A$$

and

$$L' = L'(1) \cap L'(2) \cap \cdots \subset A'$$

where $L(0) = A$, $L'(0) = A'$ and, for each $k \in N \backslash \{0\}$,

$$L(k+1) = V(L'(k))$$

and

$$L'(k+1) = V'(L(k))$$

where V and V' are the response functions for u and u'. ∎

Example 4.4. Let

$$A = \{a, b, c\}, \ A' = \{a', b', c'\}$$

and u and u' be specified by the matrix

	a'	b'	c'
a	1, 0	1, 0	2, 1
b	2, 1	2, 2	1, 3
c	1, 0	0, 2	0, 1

Then

$$L(1) = \{a, b\}, \ L'(1) = \{b', c'\},$$

$$L(2) = \{a, b\}, \ L'(2) = \{c'\},$$

$$L(3) = \cdots = \{a\}, \ L'(3) = \cdots = \{c'\}$$

so that $L = \{a\}$ and $L' = \{c'\}$. ∎

The following proposition shows that there are always some rationalisable acts.

Proposition. The rationalisable sets $L \subset A$ and $L' \subset A'$ in the strategy problem (A, A', u, u') are nonempty. ∎

Proof. Let $L(k)$ and $L'(k)$ be the sets referred to in the definition of rationalisable sets and V and V' the response functions for u and u'. Then $L(0) = A$ and $L'(0) = A'$ are nonempty. Since $V(S')$ is nonempty if S' is nonempty and $V'(S)$ is nonempty if S is nonempty, and as

$$L(k + 1) \subset L(k)$$

and

$$L'(k + 1) \subset L'(k)$$

for all $k \in N\backslash\{0\}$, $L(k)$ and $L'(k)$ are nonempty for all $k \in N$ so that L and L' are nonempty. ∎

A choice rule is rational if the sets which it assigns to a strategy problem are its rationalisable sets.

Definition. The choice rule taking (A, A', u, u') to (C, C') is rational if $C \subset A$ and $C' \subset A'$ are the rationalisable sets in (A, A', u, u'). ∎

THE CONSISTENCY AXIOM

A set S of my acts and a set S' of Nature's acts are consistent with each other if any act that I may choose maximises my expected utility given some consistent belief about the acts that Nature may choose, and any act that Nature may choose maximises her expected utility given some consistent belief about the acts which I may choose. More precisely, S and S' are consistent if all acts in S are best responses to some probability distribution on S' and all acts in S' are best responses to some probability distribution on S.

Definition. In the strategy problem (A, A', u, u') the pair of sets $S \subset A$ and $S' \subset A'$ is consistent if $S \subset V(S')$ and $S' \subset V(S)$ where V and V' are the response functions for u and u'. ∎

Example 4.5. Let $A = \{a, b\}$, $A' = \{a', b'\}$ and u and u' be specified by the matrix

	a'	b'
a	2, 1	0, 0
b	0, 0	1, 2

Then the pairs of consistent sets are

$$(\{a\}, \{a'\}), (\{b\}, \{b'\}), (A, A').$$

(This example is sometimes referred to as the battle of the sexes.) ∎

As Example 4.5 shows, there may be many pairs of consistent sets. Indeed, if S and S' are consistent and T and T' are consistent then so are $S \cup T$ and $S' \cup T'$. The maximal consistent sets are the unions, taken pairwise, of all consistent sets. Note that as pairwise unions of consistent sets are consistent the maximal consistent sets are themselves consistent.

Definition. In the strategy problem (A, A', u, u') in which the pairs of consistent sets are

$$(S(1), S'(1)), (S(2), S'(2)), \cdots$$

the maximal consistent sets are

$$M = S(1) \cup S(2) \cup \cdots \subset A$$

and

$$M' = S'(1) \cup S'(2) \cup \cdots \subset A'. \blacksquare$$

Example 4.6 Let (A, A', u, u') be specified as in Example 4.5 (the battle of the sexes). Then the maximal consistent sets are $M = A$ and $M' = A'$. ∎

A choice rule satisfies the consistency axiom if the sets which it assigns to a strategy problem are its maximal consistent sets.

Definition. The choice rule taking (A, A', u, u') to (C, C') satisfies the consistency axiom if $C \subset A$ and $C' \subset A'$ are the maximal consistent sets in (A, A', u, u'). ∎

The following proposition shows that consistency is equivalent to rationality.

Proposition. If $L \subset A$ and $L' \subset A'$ are the rationalisable sets and $M \subset A$ and $M' \subset A'$ the maximal consistent sets in the strategy problem (A, A', u, u') then $L = M$ and $L' = M'$. ∎

Proof. Let $L(k)$ and $L'(k)$ be the sets referred to in the definition of rationalisable sets and V and V' the response functions for u and u'. As A and A' are finite and as

$$L(k + 1) \subset L(k)$$

and

$$L'(k + 1) \subset L'(k)$$

for all $k \in N \backslash \{0\}$ there is some $h \in N$ such that $L(h) = L$ and $L'(h) = L'$; then $L = V(L')$ and $L' = V(L)$ so that $L \subset V(L')$ and $L' \subset V(L)$ and thus L and L' are consistent. Hence $L \subset M$ and $L' \subset M'$. Now let S and S' be consistent. Then $S \subset L(0)$ and $S' \subset L'(0)$, trivially. Assume that $S \subset L(k)$ and $S' \subset L'(k)$ for some arbitrary $k \in N$. Then, as $S' \subset T'$ implies that $V(S') \subset V(T')$,

$$S \subset V(S') \subset V(L'(k)) = L(k + 1).$$

It follows by induction that $S \subset L(k)$ for all $k \in N$ so that $S \subset L$. Similarly, $S' \subset L'$. Since this applies for all consistent pairs S and S' it follows that $M \subset L$ and $M' \subset L'$. Hence $L = M$ and $L' = M'$. ∎

This proposition immediately leads to the following characterisation of the set of rational choice rules.

Remark. A choice rule on the family of strategy problems is rational if and only if it satisfies the consistency axiom. ∎

DOMINANCE

An alternative approach to the solution of strategy problems is provided by the concept of dominance. My act a is dominated by my act b if, whatever act is chosen by Nature, I prefer b to a: that is, a is dominated by b if

$$u(b, a') > u(a, a')$$

for all a' in A'.

Example 4.7. Let (A, A', u, u') be specified as in Example 4.1 (the prisoners' dilemma). Then a is dominated by b; and a' is dominated by b'. ■

An act may be dominated by a combination of other acts even if it is not dominated by any one act. A combination of acts in A is a list of nonnegative weights, one for each act, whose sum is unity: that is, a probability distribution on A. My expected utility obtained from the combination p on A when Nature chooses the act a' is

$$\sum p(b) \cdot u(b, a').$$

My act a is dominated by the combination p if this expected utility exceeds $u(a, a')$ for all a' in A'.

Example 4.8. Let

$$A = \{a, b, c\}, \ A' = \{a', b'\}$$

and u and u' be specified by the matrix

	a'	b'
a	0, 0	3, 2
b	1, 1	1, 1
c	3, 2	0, 0

Rational Choice

Then b is dominated by the combination p such that

$$p(a) = p(b) = 1/2$$

but is not dominated by either a or c. ∎

My act a is undominated if it is not dominated by any combination p. More generally, a is undominated for some subset S' of A' if there is no combination p such that my expected utility given p exceeds $u(a, a')$ for all a' in S'.

Definition. In the strategy problem (A, A', u, u') the act $a \in A$ is S'-undominated for u if there is no probability distribution p on A such that

$$\sum p(b) \cdot u(b, a') > u(a, a')$$

for all $a' \in S' \subset A'$; the property of being S-undominated for u' is defined analogously. ∎

The following proposition shows that if an act is a best response to some probability distribution then it is undominated. More generally, it shows that if a is a best response to a probability distribution on some subset S' of A' then a is S'-undominated.

Proposition. If in the strategy problem (A, A', u, u') $a \in A$ is a best response for u to some probability distribution on $S' \subset A'$ then a is S'-undominated for u; the corresponding implication applies for S and u'. ∎

Proof. If a is a best response to $p' \in P(S')$ then

$$\sum p'(a') \cdot u(a, a') \geq \sum p'(a') \cdot u(b, a')$$

for all $b \in A$ so that

$$\sum p'(a') \cdot u(a, a') \geq \sum p'(a') \cdot \sum p(b) \cdot u(b, a')$$

for all $p \in P(A)$. This implies that we cannot, for any $p \in P(A)$, have

$$\sum p(b) \cdot u(b,a') > u(a, a')$$

for all $a' \in S'$. It follows that a is S'-undominated. The corresponding implication for u' is demonstrated analogously. ∎

As an act must be undominated if it is to be a best response it must be undominated if it is to be rationalisable. However, an act may be undominated but not rationalisable, as the following example shows.

Example 4.9. Let

$$A = \{a,b,c\}, \ A' = \{a',b'\}$$

and u and u' be specified by the matrix

	a'	b'
a	0, 0	3, 1
b	2, 1	2, 2
c	3, 2	0, 3

Then, as may be verified, c is A'-undominated for u but is not rationalisable. ∎

ITERATIVELY UNDOMINATED ACTS

In Example 4.9 my undominated act c fails to be rationalisable because it becomes dominated if Nature's act a' is deleted from the strategy problem; and it is appropriate to delete a' because it is dominated by b'. That is, c fails to survive the iterated deletion of dominated acts.

If an act a does survive the iterated deletion of dominated acts then a is A'-undominated; we write the set of A'-undominated acts as $D(1)$, and define $D'(1)$ analogously. Further, *a* is undominated for the set of all acts for Nature which are *A*-undominated: that is, *a* is $D'(1)$-undominated, and so forth. This chain of reasoning leads to the following definition.

Definition. In the strategy problem (A, A', u, u') the iteratively undominated sets are

$$D = D(1) \cap D(2) \cap \cdots \subset A$$

and

$$D' = D'(1) \cap D'(2) \cap \cdots \subset A'$$

where $D(0) = A$, $D'(0) = A'$ and, for each $k \in N \setminus \{0\}$, $D(k + 1)$ is the set of $a \in A$ which are $D'(k)$-undominated for *u* and $D'(k + 1)$ is the set of $a' \in A'$ which are $D(k)$-undominated for u'. ∎

The following proposition shows that rationalisable acts are iteratively undominated. Since there are always some rationalisable acts this implies that there are always some undominated acts.

Proposition. If $L \subset A$ and $L' \subset A'$ are the rationalisable sets and $D \subset A$ and $D' \subset A'$ the iteratively undominated sets in the strategy problem (A, A', u, u') then $L \subset D$ and $L' \subset D'$. ∎

Proof. Let $L(k)$ and $L'(k)$ be the sets referred to in the definition of rationalisable sets and $D(k)$ and $D'(k)$ the sets referred to in the definition of iterative dominance. Then $L(0) \subset D(0)$ and $L'(0) \subset D'(0)$, trivially. Assume that $L(k) \subset D(k)$ and $L'(k) \subset D'(k)$ for some arbitrary $k \in N$. If $a \in L(k + 1)$ then $a \in V(L'(k))$, which is to say that *a* is a best response to some $p' \in P'(L'(k))$ and thus to $p' \in P'(D'(k))$ so that *a* is $D'(k)$-undominated and thus $a \in D(k + 1)$. It follows that $L(k) \subset D(k)$ for all $k \in N$ so that $L \subset D$. Similarly, $L' \subset D'$. ∎

A lengthier argument (which we do not give) shows that the converse of this proposition is also true: that is, that iteratively undominated acts are rationalisable. In fact, the lengthy part of the argument consists of showing that undominated acts are best responses; given this, the above proof can readily be reversed to show that $D \subset L$ and $D' \subset L'$.

A less restrictive property than that of dominance is that of weak dominance. My act a is weakly dominated by my act b if for some act of Nature I prefer b to a and for no act of Nature do I prefer a to b.

Example 4.10. Let $A = \{a,b\}, A' = \{a',b'\}$ and u and u' be specified by the matrix

	a'	b'
a	0, 0	1, 1
b	1, 1	2, 1

Then b dominates, and thus weakly dominates, a; and b' weakly dominates, but does not dominate, a'. ■

It might be supposed that weakly dominated acts may be iteratively deleted without affecting rationality in the same way that dominated acts may be. However, this supposition is false, as the following example shows.

Example 4.11. Let $A = \{a,b\}, A' = \{a',b'\}$ and u and u' be specified by the matrix

	a'	b'
a	0, 0	1, 1
b	1, 1	0, 1

Then, as may be verified, b is rationalisable. However, b' weakly dominates a', and if a' is deleted from the strategy problem then a dominates b. ■

EQUILIBRIUM IN BELIEFS

The dominance approach provides a solution which is no more precise than that provided by rationality. An alternative approach which provides a solution which is more precise is that of an equilibrium in beliefs (sometimes referred to as a mixed Nash equilibrium).

Rationality requires that acts are best responses to some reasoned beliefs but does not require that these beliefs are mutually correct. Equilibrium adds this requirement. More precisely, a belief for me and a belief for Nature together constitute an equilibrium in beliefs if I may choose any act to which Nature assigns positive probability and Nature may choose any act to which I assign positive probability. That is, the probability distributions p on A and p' on A' constitute an equilibrium in beliefs if each act in the support of p is a best response to p', and each act in the support of p' is a best response to p. The acts in the supports of p and p' are the equilibrium acts for me and Nature.

Definition. The probability distributions p on A with support $S \subset A$ and p' on A' with support $S' \subset A'$ constitute an equilibrium in beliefs in the strategy problem (A, A', u, u') if each $a \in S$ is a best response for u to p' and each $a' \in S'$ is a best response for u' to p; if this obtains then S and S' are the equilibrium sets corresponding to p and p'. ∎

Example 4.12. Let $A = \{a, b\}$, $A' = \{a', b'\}$ and u and u' be specified by the matrix

	a'	b'
a	1, 0	0, 1
b	0, 1	1, 0

Then p and p' where

$$p(a) = p(b) = 1/2$$

and

$$p'(a') = p'(b') = 1/2$$

constitute an equilibrium in beliefs and the corresponding equilibrium sets are A and A'. (This example is sometimes referred to as matching pennies.) ∎

The following proposition shows that equilibrium acts are rationalisable.

Proposition. If $S \subset A$ and $S' \subset A'$ are equilibrium sets and $L \subset A$ and $L' \subset A'$ the rationalisable sets in the strategy problem (A, A', u, u') then $S \subset L$ and $S' \subset L'$. ∎

Proof. Let p and p' constitute the equilibrium in beliefs corresponding to S and S'. Then $a \in S$ implies that a is a best response to some $p' \in P'(S')$: that is, $a \in V(S')$ where V is the response function for u. Thus $S \subset V(S')$. Similarly, $S' \subset V'(S)$ where V' is the response function for u'. Thus S and S' are a consistent pair so that $S \subset L$ and $S' \subset L'$. ∎

The converse of this proposition is false, as the following example shows.

Example 4.13. Let

$$A = \{a, b, c\}, \quad A' = \{a', b', c'\}$$

and u and u' be specified by the matrix

	a'	b'	c'
a	0, 7	2, 5	7, 0
b	5, 2	3, 3	5, 2
c	7, 0	2, 5	0, 7

Then, as may be verified, p and p' where $p(b) = 1$ and $p'(b') = 1$ constitute the unique equilibrium in beliefs and the corresponding equilibrium sets are $\{b\}$ and $\{b'\}$; however, the rationalisable sets are A and A'. ∎

Thus equilibrium provides a more precise solution to the strategy problem than does rationality: not only may equilibrium exclude certain rationalisable acts, it also assigns probabilities to the acts which remain. However, it is less satisfactory. As we have noted, equilibrium requires that beliefs be mutually correct. But this cannot be implied by rationality, which is essentially an individualistic rather than a mutual concept. Further, there may be more than one equilibrium in beliefs, as the following example shows. If there is then they cannot all be mutually correct.

Example 4.14. Let

$$A = \{a,b,c\}, \ A' = \{a',b'\}$$

and u and u' be specified by the matrix

	a'	b'
a	2, 1	1, 2
b	1, 2	2, 1
c	2, 0	0, 0

Then, as may be verified, p and p' where

$$p(a) = p(b) = 1/2$$

and

$$p'(a') = p'(b') = 1/2$$

constitute an equilibrium in beliefs as do q and q' where $q(c) = 1$ and $q'(a') = 1$. ∎

EQUILIBRIUM IN ACTS

A yet more precise solution is provided by the concept of an equilibrium in acts (sometimes referred to as a pure Nash equilibrium). An act a for me and an act a' for Nature together constitute an equilibrium in acts if when I choose a

there is no act which Nature prefers to a' and when Nature chooses a' there is no act which I prefer to a.

Definition. The acts $a \in A$ and $a' \in A'$ constitute an equilibrium in acts in the strategy problem (A, A', u, u') if

$$u(a, a') \geq u(b, a')$$

for all $b \in A$ and

$$u'(a, a') \geq u'(a, b')$$

for all $b' \in A'$. ∎

Example 4.15. Let (A, A', u, u') be specified as in Example 4.1 (the prisoners' dilemma). Then (b, b') is an equilibrium in acts. ∎

If a and a' constitute an equilibrium in acts and p and p' are the degenerate probability distributions which assign probabilities of 1 to a and a' then a is a best response to p' and a' is a best response to p so that p and p' constitute an equilibrium in beliefs. Thus the constituents of an equilibrium in acts are in the equilibrium sets corresponding to some equilibrium in beliefs. It follows that the constituents of an equilibrium in acts are rationalisable.

As the preceding discussion makes clear, an equilibrium in acts may be interpreted as a special case of an equilibrium in beliefs. However, the fundamental problem of equilibrium (that is, that there may be multiple inconsistent equilibria) remains, as the following example shows.

Example 4.16. Let (A, A', u, u') be specified as in Example 4.2 (meeting in New York). Then both (a, a') and (b, b') are equilibria in acts but neither (a, b') nor (a', b) is an equilibrium in acts. ∎

A yet more serious problem is that there may be no equilibrium in acts, as the following example shows.

Example 4.17. Let (A, A', u, u') be specified as in Example 4.12 (matching pennies). Then

$$u'(a, b') > u'(a, a'), \ u(b, b') > u(a, b'),$$

$$u'(b, a') > u'(b, b'), \ u(a, a') > u(b, a')$$

so that there is no equilibrium in acts. ∎

Notes

The concept of rationalisable acts is due to Bernheim (1984 and 1986) and Pearce (1984). That of dominance originates in the work of Luce and Raiffa (1957); it is developed by Moulin (1979). The concepts of equilibrium in beliefs and equilibrium in acts are, as their alternative names suggest, due to Nash (1951).

The property that undominated acts are best responses, which in turn implies that iteratively undominated acts are rationalisable, is proved, in a slightly different setting, by Ferguson with 'the help of a famous theorem – one of the great theorems of mathematics' (1967, p. 70).

Surveys covering some of the material discussed in this chapter and various extensions to this are provided by Fudenberg and Tirole (1991) and Osborne and Rubinstein (1994).

5 Knowledge

We digress from our main theme to discuss the concept of knowledge and its relation to rationality. We first discuss what it means to know something and then what it means for something to be common knowledge. We conclude by exploring the connection between knowledge and rationality.

KNOWLEDGE FUNCTIONS

The concept of knowledge involves states of the world. In Chapter 2 a state was interpreted as a description of some aspect of the physical universe. In the present context this interpretation is extended to comprise a description of the whole of the physical universe together with what I and Nature both know about the universe, what we know about what we each know, and so forth. We assume that the set S of all possible states is finite.

Knowledge is limited: I do not in general know what the prevailing state is. I do, however, know something of this state: trivially, I know that it is in S. Typically, I know that it is in some proper subset E of S: if this is the case then we say that I know the set E. Further, I know different sets in different states. Assume, for example, that I have two coins but only observe the first and consider the set of possible states

$$S = \{HH, HT, TH, TT\}$$

where HT is the state in which the first coin displays heads and the second displays tails, and so forth. If the state is HH then, as I observe that the first coin displays heads, I know that the state is either HH or HT: that is, I know the set $\{HH, HT\}$. Trivially, I also know S. Analogous observations apply in the other states. Thus I know S in all states; I know $\{HH, HT\}$ only in the states HH and HT; I know $\{TH, TT\}$ only in the states TH and TT; and I know other subsets of S in no states.

We may make the extent of my knowledge precise by specifying for each set of states E the set of states $K(E)$ in which E is known. This specification must satisfy four properties. First, something is known: S is known in all states or, $K(S) = S$. Second, knowing two things is the same as knowing both: the states in which both E is known and F is known are the same as the states in which both E and F are known or

$$K(E) \cap K(F) = K(E \cap F).$$

Third, I cannot know what is not the case: E can be known in no state which is not in E or $K(E) \subset E$. And fourth, not knowing something is the same as knowing that it is not known: the states in which E is not known are the same as the states in which it is known that E is not known or

$$S \setminus K(E) = K(S \setminus K(E)).$$

We refer to these four knowledge properties as KP1 to KP4. The function K so defined is a knowledge function.

Definition. A knowledge function K on a finite set S is a function taking each $E \subset S$ to some $K(E) \subset S$ such that, for all $E, F \subset S$:

(KP1) $K(S) = S$;

(KP2) $K(E) \cap K(F) = K(E \cap F)$;

(KP3) $K(E) \subset E$; and

(KP4) $S \setminus K(E) = K(S \setminus K(E))$. ∎

Example 5.1. Let

$$S = \{r, s, t\}$$

and K be specified by

$$K(S) = S, \ K(\{s, \ t\}) = \{s, \ t\}$$

$$K(\{r, \ s\}) = K(\{r, \ t\}) = K(\{r\}) = \{r\}$$

with $K(\{s\})$ and $K(\{t\})$ empty. Then K is a knowledge function on S. ∎

The knowledge function specified in Example 5.1 satisfies two further properties. First, if one thing implies another then knowing the former implies knowing the latter: that is, if E is a subset of F then $K(E)$ is a subset of $K(F)$. Second, knowing something is the same as knowing that it is known: that is, $K(K(E))$ is equal to $K(E)$. The following proposition shows that these two properties, which we refer to as KP5 and KP6, obtain in general.

Proposition. If K is a knowledge function on S then, for all E, $F \subset S$:

(KP5)   if $E \subset F$ then $K(E) \subset K(F)$; and

(KP6) $K(K(E)) = K(E)$. ∎

Proof. For KP5, if $E \subset F$ then

$$K(E) = K(E \cap F) = K(E) \cap K(F) \subset K(F),$$

using KP2. For KP6,

$$K(K(E)) = K(S \backslash (S \backslash K(E)))$$
$$= K(S \backslash K(S \backslash K(E))) = S \backslash K(S \backslash K(E))$$
$$= S \backslash (S \backslash K(E)) = K(E),$$

using KP4. ∎

SELF-EVIDENT SETS

As we have noted, I cannot know what is not the case: that is, $K(E) \subset E$ for any set E. If I always know the set E when it is the case (that is, if, in addition, $E \subset K(E)$) then E is self-evident.

Definition. A set $E \subset S$ is self-evident for a knowledge function K on S if $K(E) = E$. ∎

Example 5.2. Let S and K be specified as in Example 5.1. Then the sets

$\{r\}, \{s, t\}, S$

are self-evident. ∎

In Example 5.2 all sets of the form $K(E)$ are self-evident. The following proposition shows that this applies in general so that, in particular, S is self-evident; it also shows that the intersections, unions and complements of self-evident sets are self-evident.

Proposition. If H is the family of self-evident sets for a knowledge function K on S then, for all $T \subset S$ and $E, F \in H$:

(a) $K(T) \in H$;

(b) $E \cap F \in H$;

(c) $E \cup F \in H$; and

(d) $E \backslash F \in H$. ∎

Proof. For (a),

$$K(K(T)) = K(T)$$

for all $T \subset S$, by KP6, so that $K(T) \in H$. For (b), if $E, F \in H$ then

$$E \cap F = K(E) \cap K(F) = K(E \cap F),$$

by KP2, so that $E \cap F \in H$. For (c), if $E, F \in H$ then

$$E = K(E) = K(E \cap (E \cup F))$$
$$= K(E) \cap K(E \cup F) \subset K(E \cup F),$$

by KP2. Similarly, $F \subset K(E \cup F)$. Thus

$$E \cup F \subset K(E \cup F),$$

so that

$$E \cup F = K(E \cup F),$$

by KP3, and $E \cup F \in H$. For (d), if $E \in H$ then

$$S \backslash E = S \backslash K(E) = K(S \backslash K(E)),$$

by KP4, so that $S \backslash E \in H$. Further, if $F \in H$ then

$$E \backslash F = S \backslash ((S \backslash E) \cup F))$$
$$= K(S \backslash ((S \backslash E) \cup F))) = K(E \backslash F)$$

as

$$(S \backslash E) \cup F \in H.$$

Thus $E \backslash F \in H$. ■

The minimal set which is known in the state s is the intersection of all sets which are known in s. Note that as s is in all such sets this minimal set is nonempty.

Definition. If K is a knowledge function on S and $s \in S$ then

$$\cap \{ E \subset S : s \in K(E) \}$$

is the minimal s-known set for K. ■

The following proposition shows that each such minimal set is self-evident.

Proposition. If $s \in S$ and $J(s)$ is the minimal s-known set for a knowledge function K on S then $J(s)$ is self-evident for K. ∎

Proof. For each $s \in S$

$$K(J(s)) = K(\cap\{E \subset S : s \in K(E)\})$$

$$= \cap\{K(E) \subset S : s \in K(E)\}$$

$$= \cap\{F \subset S : s \in K(F)\} = J(s)$$

$$= \cap\{K(E) \subset S : s \in K(K(E))$$

by KP2 and KP6, so that $J(s)$ is self-evident. ∎

KNOWLEDGE PARTITIONS

We refer (for reasons which will become apparent) to a partition on S each element of which is associated with some state which it contains as a knowledge partition on S.

Definition. If

$$J = \{J(s) : s \in S\}$$

is a partition on S and $s \in J(S)$ for all $s \in S$ then J is a knowledge partition on S. ∎

The following proposition shows that the family of minimal known sets is a knowledge partition on S.

Proposition. If, for all $s \in S$, $J(s)$ is the minimal s-known set for a knowledge function K on S then

$$\{J(s) : s \in S\}$$

is a knowledge partition on S. ∎

Proof. Since $K(E) \subset E$, by KP3, $s \in E$ for each set E in the family whose intersection is

$$J(s) = \cap \{E \subset S : s \in K(E)\}$$

so that $\{s\} \subset J(s)$, and thus $J(s)$ is nonempty, for each $s \in S$. Then

$$S = \cup \{\{s\} : s \in S\} \subset \cup \{J(s) : s \in S\}$$

so that

$$\cup \{J(s) : s \in S\} = S.$$

Now, for all $t \in S$,

$$K(J(t)) = J(t)$$

as $J(t)$ is self-evident so that $s \in J(t)$ implies that $s \in K(J(t))$ which implies that $J(s) \subset J(t)$ which, as $J(t)$ is minimal, implies that $J(s) = J(t)$. Similarly, for all $r \in S$, $s \in J(r)$ implies that $J(s) = J(r)$. It follows that either $J(t) \cap J(r)$ is empty or $J(t) = J(r)$. Thus

$$\{J(s) : s \in S\}$$

is a partition on S and, as $s \in J(S)$ for all $s \in S$, a knowledge partition on S. ∎

Example 5.3. Let S and K be specified as in Example 5.1. Then the minimal known sets

$$J(r) = \{r\}, \ J(s) = \{s, t\}, \ J(t) = \{s, t\}$$

form a knowledge partition on S. This example is illustrated in Figure 5.1. ∎

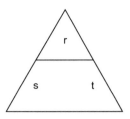

Figure 5.1

Instead of generating a knowledge partition from a knowledge function we may consider generating a knowledge function from a knowledge partition. If J is an arbitrary knowledge partition on S we may consider the states s in which the set E is known to be those whose associated partition elements $J(s)$ are contained in E: that is, we may specify that

$$K(E) = \{s \in S: J(s) \subset E\}.$$

This is equivalent to specifying that $K(E)$ is the union of all the sets $J(s)$ which are contained in E, or that

$$K(E) = \cup \{J(s): J(s) \subset E\}.$$

The following proposition shows that this specification generates a knowledge function.

Proposition. If J is a knowledge partition on S then the function K taking $E \subset S$ to

$$\{s \in S: J(s) \subset E\}$$

is a knowledge function on S. ∎

Proof. For KP1,

$$K(S) = \{s \in S: J(s) \subset S\} = S.$$

For KP2,

$s \in K(E) \cap K(F)$

if and only if $J(s) \subset E \cap F$ which obtains if and only if $s \in K(E \cap F)$. Thus

$$K(E) \cap K(F) = K(E \cap F)$$

for all $E, F \subset S$. For KP3, $s \in K(E)$ implies that $J(s) \subset E$ which implies that $s \in E$ since $s \in J(s)$. Thus $K(E) \subset E$ for all $E \subset S$. For KP4, note that if F is the union of partition elements $J(s)$ then

$$K(F) = \cup\{J(s): J(s) \subset F\} = F.$$

Then as $K(E)$ is the union of partition elements $J(s)$ so is $S \backslash K(E)$ so that

$$S \backslash K(E) = K(S \backslash K(E))$$

for all $E \subset S$. ∎

Note that the above proof also shows that a set E is self-evident if and only if it is the union of partition elements: that is, if and only if

$$E = \cup\{J(s): s \in E\} = J(E),$$

say.

Example 5.4. Let

$$S = \{r, s, t\}$$

and

$$\{\{r\}, \{s, t\}\}$$

be a knowledge partition on S. Then the function K defined by

$$K(S) = S, \ K(\{s, \ t\}) = \{s, \ t\},$$

$$K(\{r, \ s\}) = K(\{r, \ t\}) = K(\{r\}) = \{r\}.$$

with $K(\{s\})$ and $K(\{t\})$ empty (which is the function K specified in Example 5.1) is a knowledge function on S. ∎

The preceding two propositions explain why a knowledge partition is so called. They also show that there is a one-to-one correspondence between knowledge functions and knowledge partitions. This correspondence justifies the following definition.

Definition. A knowledge partition J on S is the knowledge partition corresponding to the knowledge function K on S if, for all $s \in S$ and $E \subset S$, $J(s) \subset E$ if and only if $s \in K(E)$. ∎

MUTUAL KNOWLEDGE

We have thus far been concerned only with the extent of my knowledge. We now turn to the possible connections between the extent of my knowledge and that of Nature's. We denote my and Nature's knowledge functions by K and K' and my and Nature's knowledge partitions by J and J'.

To say that in the state s I know the set E is to say that $s \in K(E)$ or, equivalently, that $J(s) \subset E$; and to say that Nature knows the set E is to say that $s \in K'(E)$ or, equivalently, that $J'(s) \subset E$. If we both know E then E is mutual knowledge in s.

Definition. The set $E \subset S$ is mutual knowledge in $s \in S$ for the knowledge functions K and K' on S if

$$s \in K(E) \cap K'(E). \ ∎$$

The remark below follows directly from this definition.

Remark. The set $E \subset S$ is mutual knowledge in $s \in S$ for the knowledge functions K and K' on S if and only if

$$J(s) \cup J'(s) \subset E$$

where J and J' are the knowledge partitions corresponding to K and K'. ■

Example 5.5. Let

$$S = \{r,\ s,\ t\},\ J = \{\{r\},\{s,\ t\}\},\ J' = \{\{r,\ s\},\{t\}\}.$$

Then

$$J(r) \cup J'(r) = \{r,\ s\}$$

so that in r the sets $\{r,s\}$ and S are mutual knowledge; similarly, in s only the set S is mutual knowledge; and in t the sets $\{s,\ t\}$ and S are mutual knowledge. This example is illustrated in Figure 5.2. ■

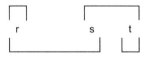

Figure 5.2

COMMON KNOWLEDGE

To say that in the state s I know that Nature knows the set E is to say that I know the set $K'(E)$, which is to say that $s \in K(K'(E))$, or, equivalently, that $J'(J(s)) \subset E$. The fact that I and Nature both know E (that is, that E is mutual knowledge) does not imply that I know that Nature knows E or that Nature knows that I know E, as the following example shows.

Example 5.6. Let S, J and J' be specified as in Example 5.5. Then $\{r,\ s\}$ is mutual knowledge in r but

$$J(J'(r)) = J(\{r,\ s\}) = \{r\} \cup \{s,\ t\} = S$$

is not contained in $\{r, s\}$. Similarly, $\{s, t\}$ is mutual knowledge in t but $J'(J(t))$ is not contained in $\{s, t\}$. ■

If, in the state s, I and Nature both know the set E, I know that Nature knows E, Nature knows that I know E, I know that Nature knows that I know E, and so forth, then E is common knowledge in s. That is, E is common knowledge in s if s is in every set of the form

$$K(K'(K \cdots K'(E) \cdots))$$

and is also in every set of the form

$$K'(K(K' \cdots K(E) \cdots)).$$

Note that as S is finite, and because of KP3, there is only a finite number of such sets. Also note that we do not need to specify that I know that I know E: that is, that $s \in K(K(E))$, and so forth. Since

$$K(K(E)) = K(E)$$

by KP6 this is ensured by the requirement that $s \in K(E)$.

Definition. A set $E \subset S$ is common knowledge in $s \in S$ for the knowledge functions K and K' on S if s is an element of each set of the form

$$K(K'(K \cdots K'(E) \cdots))$$

and each set of the form

$$K'(K(K' \cdots K(E) \cdots)). ■$$

The remark below follows directly from this definition.

Remark. A set $E \subset S$ is common knowledge in $s \in S$ for the knowledge functions K and K' if and only if each set of the form

$$J'(J(J'\cdots J(s)\cdots))$$

and each set of the form

$$J(J'(J\cdots J'(s)\cdots))$$

are subsets of E where J and J' are the knowledge partitions corresponding to K and K'. ∎

Example 5.7. Let

$$S = \{r,s,t,u\}, \ J = \{\{r,s\},\{t\},\{u\}\}, \ J' = \{\{r,s,t\},\{u\}\}.$$

Then, as may be verified, in r,s and t the sets $\{r,s,t\}$ and S are common knowledge; and in u all sets which contain u are common knowledge. This example is illustrated in Figure 5.3. ∎

The differences between mutual and common knowledge may be illustrated as follows. Assume that I and Nature each have a coin which displays heads; we can each observe our own coin but cannot observe the other's coin. A third party asks Nature and then me whether we know what the other's coin displays. Clearly, we each say that we do not. The third party then informs us that at least one of the coins displays heads and repeats the questions. Nature again says that she does not, but, on hearing this, I say that I do, since Nature's reply informs me that my coin does not display tails. Thus my response changes when I am informed of something which I already know: namely, that at least one coin displays heads. This is because the information which I receive turns mutual knowledge into common knowledge.

Figure 5.3

COMMON KNOWLEDGE AND SELF-EVIDENT SETS

While the preceding definition captures the intuitive sense of common knowledge it is cumbersome. The following proposition shows that we may equivalently define a set to be common knowledge if it has a subset which is self-evident for both me and Nature.

Proposition. A set $E \subset S$ is common knowledge in $s \in S$ for the knowledge functions K and K' on S if and only if there is some $F \subset S$ which is self-evident for K and K' and such that $s \in F \subset E$. ∎

Proof. First, let $E \subset S$ be common knowledge in s for K and K'. Then

$$s \in \cdots K'(K(E)) \subset K(E) \subset E$$

and

$$s \in \cdots K(K'(E)) \subset K'(E) \subset E,$$

by KP3. As S is finite there is some

$$F = K(K'(K \cdots K'(E) \cdots))$$

such that $K'(F) = F$. Now $s \in F \subset E$, and $K(F) = F$, by KP6, so that F is self-evident for K and K'. To prove the converse, assume that there is some F such that

$$s \in K(F) = K'(F) = F \subset E.$$

Then every set of the form

$$K(K'(K \cdots K'(E) \cdots))$$

is equal to F, by KP6, as is every set of the form

$$K'(K(K' \cdots K(E) \cdots)).$$

Also, s is in each such set, by KP5, so that E is common knowledge in s for K and K'. ∎

The remark below follows from this proposition.

Remark. A set $E \subset S$ is common knowledge in $s \in S$ for the knowledge functions K and K' if and only if there is some $F \subset S$ such that

$$s \in F = J(F) = J'(F) \subset E$$

where J and J' are the knowledge partitions corresponding to K and K'.

Example 5.8. Let S, J and J' be specified as in Example 5.7. Then

$$J(\{r,s,t\}) = J'(\{r,s,t\}) \subset \{r,s,t\}$$

so that in r, s and t the set $\{r,s,t\}$ is common knowledge, as, clearly, is S; similarly, in u all sets which contain u are common knowledge. ∎

As an application of the concept of common knowledge assume that there is a given probability distribution of S. The probability which I assign to some set E will depend on what I know: we write the probability which I assign to E when the smallest set which I know is F as $p(E;F)$. Now in the state s the smallest set which I know is $J(s)$, where J is my knowledge partition, so in this state I assign the probability $p(E;J(s))$ to the set E; similarly, Nature assigns the probability $p(E;J'(s))$, where J' is Nature's knowledge partition.

I and Nature will typically assign different probabilities to E. Indeed, it may be common knowledge that we assign different probabilities. Assume, for example, that Nature observes a coin but I do not and consider the set of possible states $S = \{H, T\}$, say, each element of which is equiprobable. In the state H I assign a probability of $1/2$ to each of the sets

$\{H\}$ and $\{T\}$ while Nature assigns a probability of 1 to the former and 0 to the latter; analogous assignments are made in state T. Thus in each state I and Nature assign different probabilities to each of the sets $\{H\}$ and $\{T\}$. This means that S is the set of states in which I and Nature assign different probabilities. Since S is common knowledge this means that it is common knowledge that we assign different probabilities.

However, although it may be common knowledge that I and Nature assign different probabilities it cannot be common knowledge that we assign different specified probabilities: that is, it cannot be common knowledge that I assign a probability of q to some set T and Nature assigns a probability of q' which differs from q. To see this note that the set E of states in which I assign the probability q to T is

$$\{s \in S : p(T; J(s)) = q\};$$

the set E' of states in which Nature assigns the probability q' to T is specified analogously. Then the set of states in which I assign the probability q and Nature assigns the probability q' is $E \cap E'$. If this set is common knowledge then there is some subset F of $E \cap E'$ which is self-evident for both me and Nature. As F is self-evident it is the union of partition elements and, as

$$F \subset E \cap E' \subset E,$$

it is the union of partition elements contained in E, that is, of sets $J(s)$ such that

$$p(T; J(s)) = q.$$

Now if C and D are two disjoint sets, the probability which we assign to T when C is the smallest set which we know is q, and the probability which we assign to T when D is the smallest set which we know is also q then the probability which we assign to T when $C \cup D$ is the smallest set which we know is yet again q. Since partition elements are disjoint it follows that $p(T; F) = q$. Similarly, $F \subset E'$ is the union of sets $J'(s)$ such that $J'(s) = q'$ so that $p(T; F) = q'$. It follows that $q = q'$. Thus it cannot be common knowledge that I and Nature assign different specified probabilities to events: we cannot agree to disagree.

KNOWLEDGE AND CHOICE PROBLEMS

The concept of knowledge illuminates a further way in which the problems of pure choice, choice under uncertainty and strategic choice are nested.

As was noted in Chapter 4, a strategy problem is specified by an array

$$H = (A, A', u, u')$$

where A and A' are nonempty finite sets and u and u' are cardinal utility functions on $A \times A'$: A and A' are the sets of acts over which I and Nature choose and u and u' represent my and Nature's preferences.

The description of a state s includes, as part of the universe, the specification of the strategy problem in s, say $H(s)$. It also includes the specification of whether Nature assigns probabilities to acts in A' and if she does the probability distribution $p'(s)$ which she adopts. Further, it includes the specification of what I know in the state: that is, my minimum known set $J(s)$ where J is my knowledge partition (and also what Nature knows, namely $J'(s)$, interpreted analogously). To specify that Nature chooses the act a' in A' is equivalent to specifying that she adopts the degenerate probability distribution $p'(s)$ which assigns the probability of 1 to a': that is, such that $p'(s)(a') = 1$.

In the problem of strategic choice I know only the strategy problem. This is to say that if the prevailing state is t then $J(t)$ is contained in the set of states s in which the strategy problem $H(s)$ is H, or

$$J(t) \subset \{s \in S: H(s) = H\} = U,$$

say. In the problem of choice under uncertainty I know, in addition, that Nature adopts the probability distribution p', so that

$$J(t) \subset \{s \in S: p'(s) = p'\} \cap U = V,$$

say. And in the problem of pure choice I further know that Nature chooses the act a', so that

$$J(t) \subset \{s \in S: p'(s)(a') = 1\} \cap V = W,$$

say.

As $W \subset V \subset U$ we thus have a hierarchy of choice problems: choice under uncertainty is a special case of strategic choice, that in which I know that Nature adopts some particular probability distribution; and pure choice is a special case of choice under uncertainty, that in which I know that the probability distribution adopted by Nature is degenerate in some particular way.

KNOWLEDGE AND RATIONALITY

We may also use the concept of knowledge to explore the connection between knowledge and rationality at its most general level: that is, in the context of strategic choice. We now consider the description of a state s to include the specification of the acts $a(s)$ and $a'(s)$ that Nature and I choose in the state.

The act that I choose coheres with what I know if it is a best response to some probability distribution on the set of Nature's acts which associates positive probability only to those acts which I know that Nature may choose: that is, to those acts in the set

$$\{a'(s) : s \in J(s)\} = a'(J(s)).$$

Equivalently, my act coheres with what I know if it is in the set $V(a'(J(s)))$, where V is my response function.

Definition. An act $a(s) \in A$, where $s \in S$, coheres with the knowledge partition J on S for u in the strategy problem (A, A', u, u') if

$$a(s) \in V(a'(J(s)))$$

where V is the response function for u (that is, for each $S' \subset A', V(S')$ is the set of $a \in A$ such that, for some probability distribution p' on S',

$$\sum p'(a') \cdot u(a, a') \geq \sum p'(a') \cdot u(b, a')$$

for all $b \in A$); coherence with J' for u' is defined analogously. ∎

To say that it is common knowledge that my and Nature's acts cohere with what we know is to say that the set of states in which our acts cohere with what we know is common knowledge in the prevailing state. The following proposition shows that if this obtains then our acts are rationalisable.

Proposition. If E is the set of $s \in S$ for which $a(s) \in A$ and $a'(s) \in A'$ cohere with the knowledge partitions J and J' on S for u and u' in the strategy problem (A, A', u, u') and E is common knowledge in $t \in S$ for the knowledge functions to which J and J' correspond then $a(t)$ and $a'(t)$ are in the rationalisable sets in (A, A', u, u'). ∎

Proof. If $a(s)$ and $a'(s)$ cohere with J and J' for u and u' then

$$a(s) \in V(a'(J(s)))$$

and

$$a'(s) \in V'(a(J'(s)))$$

where V and V' are the response functions for u and u'. Then, as E is common knowledge for J and J', there is some $F \subset S$ such that

$$t \in F = \cup\{J(s): s \in F\} = \cup\{J'(s): s \in F\} \subset E.$$

Then, for all $s \in F$, we have $J(s) \subset F$ so that

$$a'(J(s)) \subset a'(F)$$

and thus

$$V(a'(J(s))) \subset V(a'(F)).$$

Then, as

$$a(s) \in V(a'(J(s)))$$

for all $s \in F \subset E$,

$$a(s) \in V(a'(F))$$

for all $s \in F$ or, equivalently, for all $a(s) \in a(F)$ so that

$$a(F) \subset V(a'(F)).$$

Similarly,

$$a'(F) \subset V'(a(F)).$$

Thus $a(F)$ and $a'(F)$ are consistent and thus subsets of the maximal consistent sets and thus subsets of the rationalisable sets. As $t \in F$ it follows that $a(t)$ and $a'(t)$ are in the rationalisable sets. ∎

This proposition formalises the connection between knowledge and rationality: if it is common knowledge that we each act coherently then our choices are rational.

Notes

The model of knowledge presented in this chapter is due to Hintikka (1962) and Kripke (1963). The concept of common knowledge originates in the work of Lewis (1969) and is formalised by Aumann (1976). The relation between knowledge and rationality is developed by Brandenburger (1992).

Surveys covering some of the material discussed in this chapter and various extensions to this are provided by Geanakoplos (1994) and Osborne and Rubinstein (1994).

6 Society

We address the problem of social choice, as an alternative generalisation of the problem of pure choice. We first set out the problem and propose definitions of admissibility and of acceptability for social choice rules. We then characterise the acceptable rules which are reasonable and the admissible rules which are rational.

SOCIAL CHOICE PROBLEMS

We consider a society in which there are n individuals, labelled $1, \ldots, n$, the set of whom we write as N. To avoid trivialities we assume that there are at least three individuals. Each individual is able to choose rationally, in the sense developed in Chapter 1, over the finite set X of outcomes. This means that he has an ordering on X such that the set of outcomes chosen from any subset S of X is the maximal subset of S with respect to this ordering. We write individual i's ordering as $\succeq_i$. A profile for the society N is an array

$$\succeq = (\succeq_1, \cdots, \succeq_n)$$

of n orderings, one for each individual; we write the set of possible profiles for N as H.

A social choice problem is defined by a profile and a set of available outcomes. Note that a pure choice problem is the special case of a social choice problem in which there is only one individual, whose ordering remains unspecified.

Definition. A social choice problem is specified by a pair $(\succeq, S)$ where S is a nonempty subset of some fixed finite set X and $\succeq$ is in the set H of arrays $(\succeq_1, \cdots, \succeq_n)$ such that, for each i in some fixed set

Rational Choice

$$N = \{1, \cdots, n\},$$

$\succeq_i$ is an ordering on X. ∎

A choice rule for society, as any choice rule, specifies the outcomes which are chosen from each set of available outcomes. A social choice rule extends this concept: it also specifies the way in which the orderings of the individuals are taken account of, or aggregated, in the choice process. More formally, a social choice rule is a function which takes each profile and each nonempty set S of available outcomes to some nonempty subset of S.

Definition. A social choice rule (on the family of social choice problems) is a function F taking each pair $(\succeq, S)$ where $\succeq \in H$ and S is a nonempty subset of X to some nonempty $F(\succeq, S) \subset S$. ∎

Example 6.1. For each $x \in X$ let

$$v(x) = \Sigma[i \in N] \,\#\{y \in X: \ x \succ_i y\}$$

and define F by

$$F(\succeq, S) = \{x \in S: \ v(x) \geq v(y) \text{ for all } y \in S\}.$$

Then F is a social choice rule (the rank order rule). ∎

We seek to characterise the social choice rules in which the orderings of the individuals in society are aggregated in some acceptable way. There are two types of property which we might seek to invoke: information requirements, which concern the information about outcomes which is used in making social choices; and responsiveness requirements, which concern the way in which social choices respond to the orderings of the individuals in society.

INFORMATION REQUIREMENTS

The following example indicates why some information requirement is needed.

Example 6.2. Let x, y, $z \in X$ and F be the rank order rule (as defined in Example 6.1). If $\succeq$ is such that

$$x \succ_1 y \succ_1 z$$
$$z \succ_2 x \succ_2 y$$
$$x \sim_i y \sim_i z$$

for all $i > 2$ then

$$F(\succeq, \{x, z\}) = \{x, z\}$$

so that both x and z are chosen; but if $\succeq'$ is such that $x \succeq_1' z \succeq_1' y$ and $\succeq_i' = \succeq_i$ for all $i > 1$ then

$$F(\succeq', \{x, z\}) = \{z\}$$

so that only z is chosen. ■

The problem in Example 6.2 is that the social choice between the outcomes x and z changes when the profile changes in a way which does not affect any individual's ordering of these two outcomes: the social choice between x and z depends on the position of the irrelevant outcome y. To avoid such problems we require that the social choice between any two outcomes depends only on the orderings of these outcomes. This requirement is known as the independence (or independence of irrelevant alternatives) axiom.

Definition. The social choice rule F satisfies the independence axiom if, for all $\succeq, \succeq' \in H$ and x, $y \in X$, the condition $x \succeq_i y$ if and only if $x \succeq_i' y$ for all $i \in N$ implies that

$$F(\succeq, \{x, y\}) = F(\succeq', \{x, y\}). ■$$

Rational Choice

Example 6.3. Let $\succeq_0$ be some fixed ordering on X and define F by

$$F(\succeq, S) = \{x \in S : x \succeq_0 y \text{ for all } y \in S\}.$$

Then F (which is an imposed rule, with the imposed ordering $\succeq_0$) satisfies the independence axiom. ■

The independence axiom is a weak information requirement. A stronger requirement is that outcomes are treated neutrally, in that if all individuals order the outcomes x and y in the same way as they order the outcomes v and w then the social choice between x and y is the same as that between v and w. This requirement is the neutrality axiom.

Definition. The social choice rule F satisfies the neutrality axiom if, for all $\succeq, \succeq' \in H$ and

$$v, w, x, \ y \in X,$$

the conditions $x \succeq_i y$ if and only if $v \succeq'_i w$ for all $i \in N$ and $v \succeq_i w$ if and only if $x \succeq'_i \ y$ for all $i \in N$ imply that

$$F(\succeq, \{x, \ y\}) = \{x\},$$

if and only if

$$F(\succeq', \{v, \ w\}) = \{v\}. \ ■$$

Example 6.4. Let F be such that $F(\succeq, S)$ is the set of $x \in S$ for which there is no $y \in S$ such that $y \succ_i x$ for all $i \in N$. Then F (which is the unanimity, or pareto, extension rule) satisfies the neutrality axiom (and also the independence axiom). ■

The following proposition shows that neutrality implies independence.

Proposition. If a social choice rule satisfies the neutrality axiom then it satisfies the independence axiom. ■

Proof. Assume that, for all $\succeq, \succeq' \in H$ and $x, y \in X, x \succeq_i y$ if and only if $x \succeq'_i y$ for all $i \in N$. Then by neutrality, with $x = v$ and $y = w$ in the definition of this property,

$$F(\succeq, \{x, y\}) = \{x\}$$

if and only if

$$F(\succeq', \{x, y\}) = \{x\}$$

and likewise for y so that

$$F(\succeq, \{x,\ y\}) = \{x,\ y\}$$

if and only if

$$F(\succeq', \{x,\ y\}) = \{x,\ y\}$$

and thus

$$F(\succeq, \{x,\ y\}) = F(\succeq', \{x,\ y\})$$

so that the independence axiom is satisfied. ■

The converse of this proposition is false, as the following example shows.

Example 6.5. Let

$$v, w, x,\ y \in X$$

and F be an imposed rule (as defined in Example 6.3) with the imposed ordering $\succeq_0$ such that $x \succ_0 y$ and $w \succ_0 v$; note that F satisfies the independence axiom. If $\succeq$ is such that $x \succeq_i y$ and $v \succeq_i w$ for all $i \in N$ and $\succeq' = \succeq$ then

$$F(\succeq, \{x,\ y\}) = \{x\}$$

but

$$F(\succeq', \{v,\ w\}) \neq \{v\}$$

so that F does not satisfy the neutrality axiom. ∎

RESPONSIVENESS REQUIREMENTS

The following example indicates why some responsiveness requirement is needed.

Example 6.6. Let $x,\ y \in X$ and F be an imposed rule (as defined in Example 6.3) with the imposed ordering $\succeq_0$ such that $y \succ_0 x$. If $\succeq$ is such that $x \succ_i y$ for all $i \in N$ then

$$F(\succeq, \{x,\ y\}) = \{y\}$$

even though $x \succ_i y$ for all $i \in N$. ∎

The problem in Example 6.6 is that the outcome y is chosen out of x and y even though x is unanimously preferred to y. To avoid such problems we require that if one outcome is unanimously preferred to a second then it alone is chosen out of the two. Note that we do not require that the first outcome is chosen, let alone uniquely chosen, whenever it is considered to be at least as good as the second by all individuals, even if it is preferred by some. This requirement is known as the unanimity axiom (and also as the pareto axiom).

Definition. The social choice rule F satisfies the unanimity axiom if, for all $\succeq\ \in H$ and $x, y \in X$, the condition $x \succ_i y$ for all $i \in N$ implies that

$$F(\succeq, \{x,y\}) = \{x\}. \quad ∎$$

Example 6.7. Let F be specified by

$$F(\succeq, S) = \{x \in S: x \succeq_1 y \text{ for all } y \in S\}.$$

Then F (which is a dictatorial rule, with individual 1 as dictator) satisfies the unanimity axiom (and also the neutrality axiom). ∎

The unanimity axiom is a weak responsiveness requirement. A stronger requirement is that social choice should respond positively to individuals' orderings: that is, first, that there is some profile under which every outcome is chosen, and second, that if the outcome x is chosen from the outcomes x and y under one profile and x is positioned higher relative to y in a second profile then x alone is chosen under this second profile. This requirement is known as the monotonicity axiom (and also as the nonimposition with positive responsiveness axiom).

Definition. The social choice rule F satisfies the monotonicity axiom if, for all $x, y \in X$:

(a) for some $\succeq \in H$

$$F(\succeq, \{x, y\}) = \{x\}; \text{ and}$$

(b) for all $\succeq, \succeq' \in H$ the conditions $x \succ_i' y$ if $x \succ_i y$ for all $i \in N$ and $x \succeq_i' y$ if $x \sim_i y$ for all $i \in N$ and either $x \sim_j y$ and $x \succ_j' y$ for some $j \in N$ or $y \succ_j x$ and $x \sim_j' y$ for some $j \in N$ imply that if

$$x \in F(\succeq, \{x, y\})$$

then

$$\{x\} = F(\succeq', \{x, y\}). \blacksquare$$

Example 6.8. For each $x \in X$ and $S \subset X$ let

$$k(x, S) = \#\{i \in N: x \succeq_i y \text{ for all } y \in S\}$$

and let F be such that $F(\succeq, S)$ is the set of $x \in S$ such that

$$k(x, \ S) \geq k(y, \ S)$$

for all $y \in S$. Then F (which is the majority decision rule) satisfies the monotonicity axiom (and also the unanimity and neutrality axioms). ■

The following proposition shows that monotonicity implies unanimity.

Proposition. If a social choice rule satisfies the monotonicity axiom then it satisfies the unanimity axiom. ■

Proof. Let $x, y \in X$ and, using part (a) of monotonicity, let $\succeq$ be such that

$$F(\succeq, \{x, \ y\}) = \{x\}$$

and let $\succeq'$ be such that $x \succ'_i y$ for all $i \in N$. If $\succeq' = \succeq$ then unanimity is satisfied immediately; if $\succeq' \neq \succeq$ then, using part (b) of monotonicity, repeatedly if necessary, we have

$$F(\succeq', \{x, \ y\}) = \{x\}$$

so that unanimity is satisfied. ■

The converse of this proposition is false, as the following example shows.

Example 6.9. Let $x, \ y \in X$ and F be a dictatorial rule (as defined in Example 6.7) with individual 1 as dictator; note that F satisfies the unanimity axiom. If $\succeq$ is such that $x \sim_1 y$ and $y \succ_i x$ for all $i > 1$, and $\succeq'$ is such that $x \sim'_i y$ for all $i \in N$, then

$$x \in F(\succeq, \{x, \ y\})$$

but

$$\{x\} \neq F(\succeq', \{x, y\})$$

so that F does not satisfy the monotonicity axiom. ■

ADMISSIBLE AND ACCEPTABLE RULES

As we have noted, neutrality implies independence and monotonicity implies unanimity. However, the two weaker requirements, independence and unanimity, are independent of one another, as are the two stricter requirements, neutrality and monotonicity. An imposed rule satisfies the independence but not the unanimity requirement and the rank order rule satisfies the unanimity but not the independence requirement. A dictatorial rule satisfies the neutrality but not the monotonicity requirement and the rank order rule satisfies the monotonicity but not the neutrality requirement. Examples of rules which satisfy both strict, and thus both weak, requirements and of those which satisfy neither weak, and thus neither strict, requirement are obvious.

A social choice rule is admissible if it satisfies the weaker information and responsiveness requirements and is acceptable if it satisfies the stronger.

Definition. A social choice rule is admissible if it satisfies the independence and unanimity axioms; it is acceptable if it satisfies the neutrality and monotonicity axioms. ■

REASONABLE AND RATIONAL RULES

The social choice rule F is reasonable if it makes reasonable choices: that is, if, for each profile $\succeq$, the choice rule $F(\succeq, \cdot)$, which takes each nonempty subset S of X to some nonempty subset $F(\succeq, S)$ of S, is reasonable in the sense specified in

Chapter 1. It is rational if it makes rational choices: that is, if $F(\succeq,\cdot)$ is rational, again in the sense specified in Chapter 1. Thus F is reasonable if $F(\succeq,\ \cdot)$ has a reason: that is, if there is a relation $\succeq_0$ on X such that, for any nonempty subset S of X, $F(\succeq,S)$ is the maximal subset of S with respect to $\succeq_0$. Further, F is rational if this reason is transitive and thus, as any reason must be complete, an ordering. Note that, as was established in Chapter 1, if $F(\succeq,\cdot)$ does have a reason then this is its base relation.

Definition. The social choice rule F is reasonable if, for all $\succeq \in H$ and all nonempty $S \subset X, F(\succeq,S)$ is the maximal subset of S with respect to some relation $\succeq_0$ on X; F is rational if $\succeq_0$ is an ordering. ∎

It is clear that any dictatorial rule is rational. The following two examples show that the unanimity extension rule is reasonable but not rational and that the majority decision rule is not even reasonable.

Example 6.10. Let x, y, $z \in X$, F be the unanimity extension rule (as defined in Example 6.4) and $\succeq$ be such that $x \succ_1 y \sim_1 z$ and $z \succ_i x \succ_i y$ for all $i > 1$. Then

$$F(\succeq,\{x,\ y\}) = \{x\}, \ F(\succeq,\{y,\ z\}) = \{y,\ z\},$$

$$F(\succeq,\{x,\ z\}) = \{x,\ z\}$$

so that the relation $\succeq_0$ specified by

$$x \succ_0 y \sim_0 z \sim_0 x$$

is a reason for $F(\succeq,\cdot)$. Thus F is reasonable. However, $\succeq_0$ is not transitive so that F is not rational. ∎

Example 6.11. Let x, y, $z \in X$, F be the majority decision rule (as defined in Example 6.8) and $\succeq$ be such that

$$x \succ_1 y \succ_1 z$$
$$z \succ_2 x \succ_2 y$$
$$y \succ_3 z \succ_3 x$$
$$x \sim_i y \sim_i z$$

for all $i > 3$. Then

$$F(\succeq, \{x, y\}) = \{x\}, \ F(\succeq, \{y, z\}) = \{y\},$$
$$F(\succeq, \{x, z\}) = \{z\}$$

so that if $\succeq_0$ is the base relation for $F(\succeq, \cdot)$ then

$$x \succ_0 y \succ_0 z \succ_0 x$$

which implies that $F(\succeq, \{x, y, x\})$ is empty so that F is not reasonable. ∎

We have, then, weak and strict aggregation requirements (that is, admissibility and acceptability) and weak and strict consistency requirements (that is, reasonableness and rationality). We seek to characterise the social choice rules which satisfy the strict aggregation and the weak consistency requirements, and those which satisfy the weak aggregation and the strict consistency requirements. (The set of social choice rules which satisfy both weak requirements is too large to be of interest; and, as we shall see, the set of rules which satisfy both strict requirements is empty.)

ACCEPTABLE REASONABLE RULES

We start by exploring the implications of the strict aggregation and weak consistency requirements: that is, by characterising the acceptable social choice rules which are reasonable.

An individual has a veto if, for any two outcomes x and y, he can ensure that x is not rejected in the choice between x

and y. A social choice rule allows a veto if there is some such individual.

Definition. The social choice rule F allows a veto if, for all $\succeq \in H$ and $x, y \in X$, there is some $i \in N$ such that

$$x \in F(\succeq, \{x, y\})$$

whenever $x \succ_i y$. ∎

The following proposition shows that any acceptable and reasonable social choice rule must give someone a veto.

Proposition. If a social choice rule F is acceptable and reasonable then F allows a veto. ∎

Proof. If there is some individual $i \in N$ with a quasi-veto, that is, such that, for all $\succeq \in H$ and $x, y \in X$, the conditions $x \succ_i y$ and $y \succ_j x$ for all $j \neq i$ imply that

$$x \in F(\succeq, \{x, y\}),$$

then, by monotonicity, $x \succ_i y$ alone implies that

$$x \in F(\succeq, \{x, y\})$$

and then, by neutrality, $v \succ_i w$ implies that

$$v \in F(\succeq, \{v, w\})$$

for all $v, w \in X$ so that F allows a veto. Thus if F allows a veto there can be no individual with a quasi-veto. Let

$$x(1), x(2), \cdots, x(n) \in X$$

and $\succeq$ be such that

$$x(1) \succ_1 x(2) \succ_1 \cdots \succ_1 x(n)$$
$$x(2) \succ_2 x(3) \succ_2 \cdots \succ_2 x(1)$$
$$\cdots$$
$$x(n) \succ_n x(1) \succ_n \cdots \succ_n x(n-1)$$

Then

$$F(\succeq, \{x(1), x(2)\}) = \{x(1)\}$$
$$F(\succeq, \{x(2), x(3)\}) = \{x(2)\}$$
$$\cdots$$
$$F(\succeq, \{x(n), x(1)\}) = \{x(n)\}$$

because if

$$F(\succeq, \{x(1), x(2)\}) \neq \{x(1)\}$$

then

$$x(2) \in F(\succeq, \{x(1), x(2)\})$$

which would imply that individual 2 had a quasi-veto, and so forth. Thus if $\succeq_0$ is the base relation for F then

$$x(1) \succ_0 x(2) \succ_0 x(3) \succ_0 \cdots \succ_0 x(n) \succ_0 x(1)$$

which implies that

$$F(\succeq, \{x(1), x(2), \cdots, x(n)\})$$

is empty so that F is not reasonable. It follows that F must allow a veto. ∎

An individual is a quasi-dictator if, for any two outcomes x and y, he can ensure that x is not rejected in the choice between x and y (that is, he has a veto) and he can also ensure that x alone is chosen if he is weakly supported by some other individual. A social choice rule is quasi-dictatorial if there is some one such individual.

Definition. The social choice rule F is quasi-dictatorial if there is some unique $i \in N$ such that, for all $\succeq \in H$ and $x, y \in X$,

$$F(\succeq, \{x,y\}) = \{x\}$$

whenever $x \succ_i y$ and $x \succeq_j y$ for some $j \in N\setminus\{i\}$. ∎

The following proposition shows that any acceptable and reasonable social choice rule not only must give someone a veto but must also be quasi-dictatorial.

Proposition. If a social choice rule F is acceptable and reasonable then F is quasi-dictatorial. ∎

Proof. If F is acceptable and reasonable then it allows a veto. Assume that individuals 1 and 2 have a veto, let $\succeq$ be such that $x \succ_1 y$, $y \succ_2 x$ and $y \succ_3 x$ and let $\succeq'$ be such that $x \sim_3' y$ and $\succeq_i' = \succeq_i$ for all $i \neq 3$. Then, as individuals 1 and 2 have a veto,

$$F(\succeq, \{x,y\}) = \{x,y\}$$

and, by monotonicity,

$$F(\succeq', \{x,y\}) = \{x\}$$

so that individual 2 cannot have a veto. It follows that precisely one individual, say 1, has a veto. Assume that this individual is not a quasi-dictator. Then, for some $\succeq \in H$ and $x,y \in X$, there is some $i \in N\setminus\{1\}$ such that $x \succ_1 y$, $x \succeq_i y$ and

$$F(\succeq, \{x,y\}) = \{x,y\}.$$

Let $\succeq'$ be such that $x \sim_i' y$ if $x \succ_i y$, $y \succ_i' x$ if $y \sim_i x$ and $\succeq_j' = \succeq_j$ for all $j \neq i$. Then, by monotonicity,

$$F(\succeq', \{x,y\}) = \{y\}$$

so that individual 1 cannot have a veto. It follows from this contradiction that individual 1 is a quasi-dictator so that F is quasi-dictatorial. ∎

Since a quasi-dictatorial social choice rule satisfies both the neutrality and the monotonicity requirements the remark below follows from this proposition.

Remark. If F is a reasonable social choice rule then F is acceptable if and only if it is quasi-dictatorial. ∎

ADMISSIBLE RATIONAL RULES

We now turn to the implications of the weak aggregation and strict consistency requirements: that is, characterise the admissible social choice rules which are rational.

A set of individuals is quasi-decisive over the pair of outcomes x and y if x alone is chosen out of x and y whenever all individuals in the set prefer x to y and all other individuals prefer y to x. The set is decisive if, for all pairs x and y, x alone is chosen out of x and y whenever all individuals in the set prefer x to y whatever the orderings of other individuals. Note that the first property is defined in terms of some specific pair of outcomes and the second in terms of all pairs of outcomes.

Definition. The set $A \subset N$ is quasi-decisive over (x, y) where $x, y \in X$ in the social choice rule F if

$$F(\succeq, \{x, y\}) = \{x\}$$

whenever $x \succ_i y$ for all $i \in A$ and $y \succ_j x$ for all $j \in N\backslash A$; A is decisive if, for all $x, y \in X$,

$$F(\succeq, \{x, y\}) = \{x\}$$

whenever $x \succ_i y$ for all $i \in A$. ∎

The following proposition shows that in the present context if a set of individuals is quasi-decisive over some pair of outcomes then it is decisive.

Proposition. If, for some $x, y \in X, A \subset N$ is quasi-decisive over (x, y) in the admissible and rational social choice rule F then A is decisive in F. ∎

Proof. Let

$$v, w, x, y \in X$$

and $\succeq$ be such that

$$v \succ_i x \succ_i y \succ_i w$$

for all $i \in A$ and

$$y \succ_j x, \; v \succ_j x, \; y \succ_j w$$

for all $j \in N \backslash A$. Then

$$F(\succeq, \{x, y\}) = \{x\}$$

as A is quasi-decisive over (x, y). Also,

$$F(\succeq, \{v, x\}) = \{v\}$$

and

$$F(\succeq, \{y, w\}) = \{y\}$$

by unanimity. Thus if $\succeq_0$ is the (transitive) base relation for F then

$$v \succ_0 x \succ_0 y \succ_0 w$$

so that

$$F(\succeq, \{v, w\}) = \{v\}.$$

As $v \succ_i w$ for all $i \in A$ but the orderings of v and w for all individuals in $N \backslash A$ are not specified, and using independence, A is decisive. ∎

The next proposition shows that in the present context if a nonsingleton set A of individuals is decisive then so is some proper subset of A.

Proposition. If F is an admissible and rational social choice rule and the nonsingleton subset A of N is decisive in F then some proper subset of A is decisive in F. ∎

Proof. Let $\{D, E\}$ be a partition on A and $\succeq$ be such that, for some $x, y, z \in X$,

$$x \succ_i y \succ_i z$$
$$y \succ_j z \succ_j x$$
$$z \succ_k x \succ_k y$$

for all $i \in D$, $j \in E$ and $k \in N \backslash A$. Then as A is decisive

$$F(\succeq, \{y, z\}) = \{y\}$$

so that if $\succeq_0$ is the base relation for F then $y \succ_0 z$. As $\succeq_0$ is transitive this implies that either $x \succ_0 z$ or $y \succ_0 x$ so that either

$$F(\succeq, \{x, z\}) = \{x\}$$

or

$$F(\succeq, \{y, x\}) = \{y\}.$$

If the first alternative holds then D is decisive over (x, z) and so is decisive; and if the second holds then E is decisive over (y, x) and so is decisive. ∎

A social choice rule is dictatorial if it is a dictatorship rule: that is, if some individual is decisive.

Definition. The social choice rule F is dictatorial if some singleton subset of N is decisive in F. ■

The following proposition shows that any admissible and rational social choice rule must be dictatorial.

Proposition. If a social choice rule F is admissible and rational then F is dictatorial. ■

Proof. Because of unanimity N is decisive. As there is a decisive proper subset of any nonsingleton subset of N and as N is finite, some singleton subset of N must be decisive. ■

Since a dictatorial social choice rule clearly satisfies the independence and unanimity requirements the remark below follows from this proposition.

Remark. If F is a rational social choice rule then F is admissible if and only if it is dictatorial. ■

Since a dictatorial social choice rule does not satisfy the monotonicity requirement we have, in conclusion, the following important remark.

Remark. No acceptable social choice rule which is rational. ■ *There is no*

Notes

The axiomatic analysis of social choice originates in the work of Arrow (1951); this work develops the various aggregation axioms discussed in this chapter.

The discussion of reasonable choice draws on the analysis of Blau and Deb (1977) and of Bordes and Salles (1978). The organisation of the discussion of rational choice follows that of Allingham (1983), which in turn draws on that of Blau (1972).

Surveys covering some of the material discussed in this chapter and various extensions to this are provided by Suzumura (1983) and Sen (1986).

Appendix: Sets and Numbers

This appendix presents an outline of all the set and number theory which is used in this book. Its purpose is to provide a concise point of reference, particularly for terms which may be used with different meanings elsewhere, rather than a detailed exposition. All the symbols which are used in this appendix, other than the letters of the alphabet, are used with the same meanings throughout the book.

We assume an intuitive understanding of what a set is and the primitive concept of belonging to a set. We also assume an intuitive understanding of identity, or of what it means for two objects to be the same. Then we have two basic types of sentence: assertions of belonging, such as x belongs to S; and assertions of identity, such as x is the same as y. All other sentences may be constructed from such atomic sentences by the repeated use of the standard logical connectives of negation, conjunction and existential quantification: that is, using the phrases 'not', 'and' and 'for some'. Note that other familiar logical connectives, embodied in phrases such as 'or' (which is used in its inclusive sense), 'implies', 'if and only if' and 'for all' may be constructed from the basic three. To give but one example, 'A or B' means 'not (not A and not B)': that is, the sentence 'A or B' is true if and only if the sentence 'not (not A and not B)' is true.

If an object x belongs to a set S then we write $x \in S$ and say that x is an *element* of, or is in, S; if x is not in S then we write $x \notin S$. Note that the elements of S may themselves be sets; if they are then we sometimes refer to S as a *family*.

If the objects x and y are the same then we say that they are *equal* and write $x = y$; if they are not equal then we write $x \neq y$. The sets S and T are equal if and only if they have the same elements, in which case we write $S = T$; if S and T are not equal then we write $S \neq T$. If every element of S is an element of T then we write $S \subset T$ and say that S is a *subset* of, or is contained in, T. Note that $S \subset T$ is consistent with $S = T$; if $S \subset T$ but $S \neq T$ then S is a *proper subset* of T. Also note that containment and belonging are conceptually different properties: for example, $S \subset S$ is always true but $S \in S$ is not.

A sentence in which the object x is free is one in which x occurs at least once without being qualified by the phrase 'for some', or by phrases from which this phrase can be derived; we write such a sentence as $L(x)$. Then we write the set whose elements are the members x of some set S for which the sentence $L(x)$ is true as

$$\{x \in S: L(x)\}.$$

If the sentence $L(x)$ is such that all the objects x which are specified by $L(x)$ being true constitute a set then we write this set as $\{x: L(x)\}$. Note that not all such sentences have this property: for example, although the sentence '$x \notin x$' is meaningful the objects x for which it is true do not constitute a set.

We can now identify a number of sets. The set $\{x: x \neq x\}$ is *empty*: that is, contains no elements. Note that there is only one empty set; any other set is said to be nonempty. The set $\{x: x = y\}$ is *singleton*: that is, contains precisely one element, namely y; we write this set as $\{y\}$. The set

$$\{x: x = y \text{ or } x = z\}$$

where $y \neq z$ contains precisely two elements, namely y and z; we write this set as $\{y, z\}$. Note that

$$\{y, z\} = \{z, y\}.$$

Sets with more than two elements may be constructed analogously.

The *union* of a family F, which we write as $\cup F$, is the set comprising all the objects which are in some element of the family: that is,

$$\{x: x \in S \text{ for some } S \in F\}.$$

If the family consists of only two sets, S and T, then we write the union as $S \cup T$. Note that x is in $S \cup T$ if and only if x is in S or T.

Analogously, the *intersection* of a (nonempty) family F, which we write as $\cap F$, is the set comprising all the objects which are in all elements of the family: that is,

$$\{x: x \in S \text{ for all } S \in F\}.$$

If the family consists of only S and T then we write the intersection as $S \cap T$. Note that x is in $S \cap T$ if and only if x is in S and T. If $S \cap T$ is empty then S and T are *disjoint*; if all pairs of sets in a family are disjoint then the family is disjoint.

A *partition* on a set S is a disjoint family of nonempty subsets of S whose union is S. Note that each element of S is in precisely one member of the partition.

The *difference* between the two sets S and T, which we write as $S \backslash T$, is the set comprising all objects which are in S but not in T: that is,

$$\{x \in S: x \notin T\}.$$

Note that this definition does not require that $T \subset S$.

The concept of the (ordered) *pair* 'x then y', which we write as (x, y), is intuitive. It may be formalised by identifying (x, y) with the set

$$\{\{x\}, \{x, y\}\}.$$

The pairs (x, y) and (u, v) are equal if and only if $x = u$ and $y = v$. Note that in general

$$(x, y) \neq (y, x).$$

Arrays with more than two components are defined analogously.

The (cartesian) *product* of the two sets S and T, which we write as $S \times T$, is the set of all pairs the first of which is in S and the second in T: that is,

$$\{(x, y) : x \in S \text{ and } y \in T\}.$$

A (binary) *relation* on a set S is a relation in which any two elements of S may, or may not, stand: for example, if x and y are in S then it may, or may not, be that $x = y$ so that $=$ is a relation on S. More formally, the relation $\succeq$ on S is a subset of $S \times S$: if $(x, y) \in \succeq$ then we write $x \succeq y$. The relation $\succeq$ is *complete* if it always stands in at least one direction: that is, if, for all x and y in S, $x \succeq y$ or $y \succeq x$. It is *transitive* if it follows through: that is, if, for all x, y and z in S, $x \succeq y$ and $y \succeq z$ imply that $x \succeq z$. A relation which is complete and transitive is an *ordering*.

The *symmetric component* $\sim$ of the relation $\succeq$ on S is the set

$$\{(x, y) \in S: x \succeq y \text{ and } y \succeq x\};$$

if $(x, y) \in \sim$ then we write $x \sim y$. The *asymmetric component* $\succ$ of $\succeq$ is the set

$$\{(x, y) \in S: x \succeq y \text{ and not } y \succeq x\};$$

if $(x, y) \in \succ$ then we write $x \succ y$. The relation $\succeq$ is (triple) *acyclic* if its asymmetric component has no minimal cycles: that is, if there are no x, y and z in S such that $x \succ y$, $y \succ z$ and $z \succ x$. A relation which is complete and acyclic is a *quasi-ordering*. Note that if a relation is an ordering then it is a quasi-ordering, but not conversely.

A *function* f from a set S to a set T is a rule which associates with each element in S some unique element in T. More formally, f is a subset of $S \times T$ with the property that if $(x, y) \in f$ and $(x, z) \in f$ then $y = z$. If $(x, y) \in f$ then we write $y = f(x)$ and say that f takes x to y. If g is a function from T to a set U then the composite function gf from S to U is defined by

$$gf(x) = g(f(x)).$$

If $V \subset S$ (and $V \nsubseteq S$) then we write the set

$$\{f(x) : x \in V\}$$

as $f(V)$. If $f(S) = T$ and f takes distinct elements in S to distinct elements in T (that is, if $f(x) = f(y)$ implies that $x = y$) then f is a *one-to-one correspondence* between S and T.

The concept of the *natural numbers*, such as 0, 1 and 2, is intuitive. It may be formalised as follows. For any set S define the successor S' of S to be the set $S \cup \{S\}$. Now identify the number 0 with the empty set, the number 1 with the set $0' = \{0\}$, the number 2 with the set $1' = \{0,1\}$ and so forth. We write the set of natural numbers as $\mathbb{N}$.

Addition and multiplication on $\mathbb{N}$ are also intuitive. *Addition* is the function taking the pair (m,n) in $\mathbb{N} \times \mathbb{N}$ to $m + n$ in $\mathbb{N}$; it is defined inductively by specifying that, for all m in $\mathbb{N}$,

$$m + 0 = m$$
$$m + 1 = (m + 0)'$$
$$m + 2 = (m + 1)'$$

and so forth. *Multiplication* is the function taking the pair (m,n) in $\mathbb{N} \times \mathbb{N}$ to $m \cdot n$ in $\mathbb{N}$; this is defined inductively by specifying that, for all m in $\mathbb{N}$,

$$m \cdot 0 = 0$$
$$m \cdot 1 = m \cdot 0 + m$$
$$m \cdot 2 = m \cdot 1 + m$$

and so forth.

If m and n are in $\mathbb{N}$ and $m = n + k$ for some k in $\mathbb{N}$ then we write $m \geq n$ and say that m is *at least as great* as n; if $m \geq n$ and $m \neq n$ then we write $m > n$ and say that m is *greater* than n. Note that $=$ and $>$ are the symmetric and asymmetric components of the relation $\geq$ on $\mathbb{N}$.

The concept of the (nonnegative) *rational numbers*, such as 1/2, 2/3 and 3/2, is also intuitive. It may be formalised by identifying such numbers with pairs of the form (m,n) where m and n are in $\mathbb{N}$ and $n \neq 0$. We write the set of such numbers as $\mathbb{Q}$. We define the relation $\geq$ on $\mathbb{Q}$ by

$$(m,n) \geq (p,q)$$

if and only if $m \cdot q \geq n \cdot p$; its symmetric and asymmetric components = and > are defined analogously.

Addition and multiplication on $\mathbb{Q}$ are derived from the corresponding operations on $\mathbb{N}$:

$$(m,n) + (p,q) = (m \cdot q + n \cdot p, \; n \cdot q)$$

and

$$(m,n) \cdot (p,q) = (m \cdot p, \; n \cdot q).$$

Subtraction and division on $\mathbb{Q}$ are the inverses of addition and multiplication, respectively. *Subtraction* is the function taking (x,y) in $\mathbb{Q} \times \mathbb{Q}$ where $x \geq y$ to $x - y$ in $\mathbb{Q}$; it is defined by $x - y = z$ where $z \in \mathbb{Q}$ is such that $x = y + z$. *Division* is the function taking (x,y) in $\mathbb{Q} \times \mathbb{Q}$ where $y \neq 0$ to x/y in $\mathbb{Q}$; it is defined by $x/y = z$ where $z \in \mathbb{Q}$ is such that $x = y \cdot z$.

Although $\mathbb{N}$ is not a subset of $\mathbb{Q}$ there is a one-to-one correspondence between the subset of $\mathbb{Q}$ which consists of all the rational numbers of the form $(m, 1)$ and $\mathbb{N}$, namely, the function which takes $(m, 1)$ to m. Accordingly, we write the rational number $(m, 1)$ as m, and, since

$$m/n = (m, 1)/(n, 1) = (m, n),$$

write the rational number (m, n) as m/n.

A set which is a subset of $\mathbb{Q}$ is the (closed rational) *unit interval*: that is, the set of all rational numbers which are not greater than 1, or

$$\{x \in \mathbb{Q}: 1 \geq x\}.$$

We write this set as $\mathbb{I}$.

The set S is *finite* if there is a one-to-one correspondence between S and some subset

$$\{1, 2, \cdots, m\}$$

of $\mathbb{N}$; if this obtains then the number of elements in, or the cardinality of, S, which we write as $\# S$, is m. If S is not finite then it is infinite. The set S is *countable* if there is a one-to-one correspondence between S and $\mathbb{N}$. Note that the sets $\mathbb{N}$, $\mathbb{Q}$ and $\mathbb{I}$ are countable but the set of all subsets of $\mathbb{N}$ (or of $\mathbb{Q}$ or of $\mathbb{I}$) is infinite but not countable.

If S is a set with m elements where $m > 1$ we may write S as

$$\{x(1), \cdots, x(m)\}.$$

Note that addition on $\mathbb{Q}$ is associative: that is, that

$$(x + y) + z = x + (y + z)$$

for all x, y and z in $\mathbb{Q}$; we write this repeated sum as $x + y + z$. Then if f is a function from S to $\mathbb{Q}$ we write

$$f(x(1)) + \cdots + f(x(m))$$

as

$$\sum [x \in S] \ f(x),$$

or, if there is no potential confusion, as $\sum f(x)$.

If $a \in \mathbb{Q}$ and f and g are functions from a set S to $\mathbb{Q}$ then so is the function h defined by

$$h(x) = a \cdot f(x) + (1 - a) \cdot g(x)$$

for all $x \in S$; in this case we write

$$h = a \cdot f + (1 - a) \cdot g.$$

If S is a nonempty set a (simple rational) *probability distribution* on S is a function p from S to $\mathbb{I}$ such that the set

$$H(p) = \{x \in S: p(x) > 0\},$$

which is the *support* of p, is finite and

$$\sum [x \in H(p)] \ p(x) = 1.$$

Appendix: Sets and Numbers

We write the *degenerate* probability distribution p such that $p(x) = 1$ for some $x \in S$ as $[x]$. If $a \in \mathbb{I}$ and p and q are probability distributions on S then so is

$$r = a \cdot p + (1-a) \cdot q;$$

we write this *compound* probability distribution as $< p, q, a >$.

The framework of this appendix is that of Frege, who has rightly been called the founding figure of analytical philosophy; it is set out in his seminal work *The Foundations of Arithmetic* (1980 translation). The exposition of this appendix draws on that of Halmos (1960). A more detailed treatment of set theory is provided by Quine (1963) and that of number theory by Cohen and Ehrlich (1963).

References

ALLINGHAM, M. (1983), *Value* (London: Macmillan).

ANSCOMBE, F. J. and AUMANN, R. J. (1963), 'A definition of subjective probability', *Annals of Mathematical Statistics*, 34: 199–205.

ARISTOTLE (1980), *The Nicomachean Ethics* (translators D. Ross, J. L. Ackrill and J. O. Urmson) (Oxford: Oxford University Press).

ARROW, K. J. (1951), *Social Choice and Individual Values* (New York: Wiley).

ARROW, K. J. (1959), 'Rational choice functions and orderings', *Economica*, NS 26: 121–7.

ARROW, K. J. (1967), 'Public and private values', in *Human Values and Economic Policy* (editor S. Hook) (New York: New York University Press).

ARROW, K. J. (1971), *Essays on the Theory of Risk-Bearing* (Amsterdam: North-Holland).

AUMANN, R. J. (1976), 'Agreeing to disagree', *Annals of Statistics*, 4: 1236–9.

BERNHEIM, B. D. (1984), 'Rationalizable strategic behavior', *Econometrica*, 52: 1007–28.

BERNHEIM, B. D. (1986), 'Axiomatic characterization of rational choice in strategic environments', *Scandinavian Journal of Economics*, 88: 473–88.

BLAIR, D. H., BORDES G., KELLY J. S. and SUZUMURA K. (1976), 'Impossibility theorems without collective rationality', *Journal of Economic Theory*, 13: 361–79.

BLAU, J. H. (1972), 'A direct proof of Arrow's theorem', *Econometrica*, 40: 61–7.

BLAU, J. H. and DEB, R. (1977), 'Social decision functions and the veto', *Econometrica*, 45: 871–9.

BORDES, G. and SALLES, M. (1978), 'Sur l'impossibilité des fonctions de décision collective', *Revue d'Economie Politique*, 88: 442–8.

BRANDENBURGER, A. (1992), 'Knowledge and equilibrium in games', *Journal of Economic Perspectives*, 6: 83–101.

CHERNOFF, H. (1954), 'Rational selection of decision functions', *Econometrica*, 22: 422–43.

COHEN, L. W. and EHRLICH, G. (1963), *The Structure of the Real Number System* (Princeton, NJ: Van Nostrand).

DEBREU, G. (1984), 'Economic theory in the mathematical mode', *American Economic Review*, 74: 267–78.

137

FERGUSON, T. S. (1967), *Mathematical Statistics* (New York: Academic Press).

FISHBURN, P. C. (1970), *Utility Theory for Decision Making* (New York: Wiley).

FREGE, G. (1980), *The Foundations of Arithmetic* (translator J. L. Austin) (Oxford: Basil Blackwell).

FUDENBERG, D. and TIROLE, J. (1991), *Game Theory* (Cambridge, MA: MIT Press).

GEANAKOPLOS, J. (1994), 'Common knowledge', in *Handbook of Game Theory* (Volume II, editors R. J. Aumann and S. Hart) (Amsterdam: North-Holland).

HALMOS, P. (1960), *Naive Set Theory* (Princeton, NJ: Van Nostrand).

HERZBERGER, H. G. (1973), 'Ordinal preference and rational choice', *Econometrica*, 41: 187–237.

HINTIKKA, J. (1962), *Knowledge and Belief* (Ithaca, NY: Cornell University Press).

HOUTHAKKER, H. S. (1950), 'Revealed preference and the utility function', *Economica*, NS 17: 159–74.

HUME, D. (1740), *A Treatise of Human Nature* (London: Noon).

KREPS, D. M. (1988), *Notes on the Theory of Choice* (Boulder, CO: Westview).

KRIPKE, S. (1963), 'Semantical analysis of model logic', *Zeitschrift für Mathematische Logik und Grundlager der Mathematik*, 9: 67–96.

LEWIS, D. K. (1969), *Convention* (Cambridge, MA: Harvard University Press).

LUCE, R. D. and RAIFFA, H. (1957), *Games and Decisions* (New York: Wiley).

MOULIN, H. (1979), 'Dominance solvable voting schemes', *Econometrica*, 47: 1337–51.

NASH, J. F. (1951), 'Non-cooperative games', *Annals of Mathematics*, 54: 286–95.

von NEUMANN, J. and MORGENSTERN, O. (1944), *Theory of Games and Economic Behavior* (Princeton, NJ: Princeton University Press).

OSBORNE, M. J. and RUBINSTEIN, A. (1994), *A Course in Game Theory* (Cambridge, MA: MIT Press).

PEARCE, D. G. (1984), 'Rationalizable strategic behavior and the problem of perfection', *Econometrica*, 52: 1029–50.

PRATT, J. W. (1964), 'Risk aversion in the small and in the large', *Econometrica*, 32: 122–36.

QUINE, W. V. O. (1963), *Set Theory and its Logic* (Cambridge, MA: Harvard University Press).

RAMSEY, F. P. (1931), 'Truth and probability', in *The Foundations of Mathematics* (editor R. B. Braithwaite) (London: Kegan Paul).

REID, C. (1970), *Hilbert* (Berlin: Springer-Verlag).

SAMUELSON, P. A. (1947), *Foundations of Economic Analysis* (Cambridge, MA: Harvard University Press).
SARIN, R. and WAKKER, P. (1997), 'A single-stage approach to Anscombe and Aumann's expected utility', *Review of Economic Studies*, 64: 399–409.
SAVAGE, L. J. (1954), *Foundations of Statistics* (New York: Wiley).
SEN, A. K. (1969), 'Quasi-transitivity, rational choice and collective decision', *Review of Economic Studies*, 36: 381–93.
SEN, A. K. (1986), 'Social choice theory', in *Handbook of Mathematical Economics* (Volume III, editors K. J. Arrow and M. D. Intrilligator) (Amsterdam: North-Holland).
SEN, A. K. (1997), 'Maximization and the act of choice', *Econometrica*, 65: 745–79.
SUZUMURA, K. (1983), *Rational Choice, Collective Decisions, and Social Welfare* (Cambridge: Cambridge University Press).

Index

Allingham, M., 128
Anscombe, F. J., 52
Aristotle, 1
Arrow, K. J., 4, 17, 28, 29, 69, 128
Aumann, R. J., 52, 109

Base relations, 11
Bentham, J., 1
Bernheim, B. D., 88
Best responses, 72, 73, 80, 84
Blair, D. H., 29
Blau, J. H., 128
Bordes, G., 29, 128
Brandenburger, A., 109

Cardinal utility functions, 34, 35,
  41, 72
Chernoff, H., 13, 29
Cohen, L. N., 136
Coherent acts, 107
Common knowledge, 100, 102, 103,
  107
Congruence axiom, 17, 19, 21
Consistency axiom, 77, 78
Consistent sets, 76, 77
Continuity axiom, 41, 43, 44, 45,
  46, 54
Contraction axiom, 13, 14, 15, 17,
  24, 26
Covering property, 54

Deb, R., 128
Debreu, G., 5
Decisive sets, 125, 126, 127, 128

Ehrlich, G., 136
Equilibrium
  in acts, 87
  in beliefs, 84
  sets, 84, 85
Expansion axiom, 13, 14, 15, 17, 26

Expected utility property, 34, 35,
  44, 45
Extension axiom, 22, 24, 26

Ferguson, T. S., 88
Fishburn, P. C., 29, 52
Frege, G., 136
Fudenberg, D., 88
Functions, 132

Geanakoplos, J., 109

Halmos, P., 136
Herzberger, H. G., 28
Hilbert, D., 5
Hintikka, J., 109
Houthakker, H. S., 20, 29
Hume, D., 1

Independence axiom, 113, 115, 119
Iteratively undominated sets, 82

Kelly, J. S., 29
Knowledge functions, 90, 91, 96, 98
Knowledge partitions, 94, 95, 96,
  98, 100, 103
Kreps, D. M., 52, 69
Kripke, S., 109

Lewis, D. K., 109
Luce, R. D., 52, 88

Maximal consistent sets, 77, 78
Maximal subsets, 9, 10, 120
Mill, J. S., 1
Minimal known sets, 93, 94
Monotone property, 54
Monotonicity axiom, 117, 118, 119
Morgenstern, O., 4, 52
Moulin, H., 88
Mutual knowledge, 98, 99

141

Nash, J. F., 4, 84, 86, 88
Neumann, J. von, 4, 52
Neutrality axiom, 114, 115, 119
Number lotteries, 53
Numbers
  addition, 132
  at least as great, 132
  division, 134
  greater, 133
  multiplication, 132
  natural, 132
  rational, 133
  subtraction, 134
  unit interval, 134

One-to-one correspondences, 132
Osborne, M. J., 88, 109
Outcome risk premiums, 61, 63, 64, 68

Pearce, D. G., 88
Pratt, J. W., 69
Probability distributions
  compound, 136
  defined, 135
  degenerate, 136
  support, 135
Probability risk premiums, 59, 61, 63, 65, 66
Pure choice problems, 8
Pure choice rules
  defined, 8
  rational, 16, 19, 22, 24, 28
  reasonable, 10, 11, 14, 15

Quasi-decisive sets, 125, 126
Quine, W. V. O., 136

Raiffa, H., 52, 88
Ramsey, F. P., 52
Rationalisable sets, 74, 75, 76, 78, 82, 85, 107
Reasons, 10, 11, 16, 28, 35, 46
Regular orderings, 54
Reid, C., 5
Relations
  acyclic, 132
  asymmetric components, 132
  complete, 132

defined, 132
orderings, 132
quasi-orderings, 132
symmetric components, 132
transitive, 132
Response functions, 73
Revealed preference axiom, 20, 21, 22
Risk aversion
  binary, 57, 61
  defined, 56, 57, 61, 64
  relative, 64, 65, 66, 68
Rubinstein, A., 88, 109

Salles, M., 128
Samuelson, P. A., 4
Sarin, R., 52
Savage, L. J., 28, 52
Self-evident sets, 92, 94, 102
Sen, A. K., 13, 22, 28, 29, 128
Sets
  countable, 135
  differences, 131
  disjoint, 131
  elements, 129
  empty, 130
  equality (of elements), 129
  families, 129
  finite, 134
  intersections, 131
  pairs (of elements) 131
  partitions, 131
  products, 131
  proper subsets, 130
  singleton, 130
  subsets, 130
  unions, 130
Social choice problems, 111
Social choice rules
  acceptable, 119, 122, 124, 125, 128
  admissible, 119, 126, 127, 128
  defined, 112
  dictatorial, 128
  quasi-dictatorial, 123, 124, 125
  rational, 120, 126, 127, 128
  reasonable, 120, 122, 124, 125
  veto allowing, 122

Strategy choice rules
    defined, 72
    rational, 76, 78
Strategy problems, 72
Substitution axiom, 37, 38, 39, 41,
    43, 44, 45, 46, 54
Suzumura, K., 29, 128

Tirole, J., 88

Unanimity axiom, 116, 118, 119
Uncertainty choice rules
    defined, 33
    rational, 34, 35, 46
Uncertainty problems, 33
Undominated acts, 80, 82
Utility representation, 26, 27, 28, 43

Wakker, P., 52